KB084574

TOEFL® MAP

New TOEFL® Edition

Speaking

Basic

DARAKWON

TOEFL® MAP

MAP New TOEFL® Edition

Speaking Basic

Publisher Chung Kyudo
Editors Zong Ziin, Cho Sangik
Authors Shane Spivey, Jonathan S. McClelland
Proofreader Michael A. Putlack
Designers Park Narae, Yoon Hyunju

First published in June 2022
By Darakwon, Inc.
Darakwon Bldg., 211, Munbal-ro, Paju-si, Gyeonggi-do 10881
Republic of Korea
Tel: 82-2-736-2031 (Ext. 250)
Fax: 82-2-732-2037

ISBN 978-89-277-8028-1 14740
       978-89-277-8025-0 14740 (set)

www.darakwon.co.kr

Photo Credits
Shutterstock.com

Components Main Book / Scripts and Answer Key
8 7 6 5 4 3 2   24 25 26 27 28

Introduction

Studying for the TOEFL® iBT is no easy task and is not one that is to be undertaken lightly. It requires a great deal of effort as well as dedication on the part of the student. It is our hope that, by using *TOEFL® Map Speaking Basic* as either a textbook or a study guide, the task of studying for the TOEFL® iBT will become somewhat easier for the student and less of a burden.

Students who wish to excel on the TOEFL® iBT must attain a solid grasp of the four important skills in the English language: reading, listening, speaking, and writing. The Darakwon *TOEFL® Map* series covers all four of these skills in separate books. There are also three different levels in all four topics. This book, *TOEFL® Map Speaking Basic*, covers the speaking aspect of the test at the basic level. With this book, students will be able to listen to lectures and conversations, read academic passages, learn vocabulary and expressions, and study topics that appear on the TOEFL® iBT.

TOEFL® Map Speaking Basic was designed both for use in a classroom setting and as a study guide for individual learners. For this reason, it offers a complete overview of the TOEFL® iBT Speaking section. Particularly, in Part B, learners are presented with passages, lectures, and conversations similar to those on the TOEFL® iBT. The topics presented in this book are based on extensive research of actual test topics. In addition, each task contains exercises and questions that help students learn to master the skills needed for that task. A sample response is provided for comparison, which helps learners develop a better understanding of how to form their own responses. As students progress through each chapter, they should become more comfortable with each task and eventually develop all of the skills they need to master the TOEFL® iBT.

In addition, *TOEFL® Map Speaking Basic* was further designed with all aspects of the student's performance in mind. The material found in these pages can prepare students to approach the TOEFL® iBT confidently and to achieve superior results. However, despite the valuable information within this book, nothing can replace hard work and dedication. In order to get the most benefit from studying *TOEFL® Map Speaking Basic*, the student must strive to do his or her best on every task in every chapter. We wish you luck in your study of both English and the TOEFL® iBT, and we hope that you are able to use *TOEFL® Map Speaking Basic* to improve your abilities in both.

Shane Spivey
Jonathan S. McClelland

TABLE
OF
CONTENTS

How Is This Book Different?   6
How to Use This Book   7

Part A | Understanding Speaking Question Types

Introduction 01   Independent Speaking   12
Introduction 02   Integrated Speaking   14
Introduction 03   Test Overview and Rubrics   23

Part B | Building Knowledge & Skills for the Speaking Test

Chapter 01

Independent Speaking

Task 1 Children Should Receive Money for Chores   26

Integrated Speaking

Task 2 Library to Reduce Book Collection   30
Task 3 Statistics: Sampling Bias   33
Task 4 Plant Biology: Trees Shedding Leaves   36

Chapter 02

Independent Speaking

Task 1 Deciding on a Teacher to Hire   40

Integrated Speaking

Task 2 University Housing Policy Change   44
Task 3 Business: Promotions   47
Task 4 Animal Science: Display Behavior   50

Chapter 03

Independent Speaking

Task 1 Taking Notes in Class vs. Concentrating on Lectures   54

Integrated Speaking

Task 2 Loaning Laptops to Students   58
Task 3 Education: Teaching Students to Follow the Rules   61
Task 4 History: The American Industrial Revolution   64

Chapter 04

Independent Speaking

Task 1 Educational Programs vs. Entertainment Programs   68

Integrated Speaking

Task 2 Adding Kitchens to Dormitories   72

Task 3 Psychology: Anchoring Bias   75

Task 4 Human Biology: Different Types of Tears   78

Chapter 05

Independent Speaking

Task 1 Spending Vacations at Home vs. Traveling   82

Integrated Speaking

Task 2 School Newspaper No Longer to Be Printed   86

Task 3 Animal Science: Echolocation   89

Task 4 Business: Ineffective Logos   92

Chapter 06

Independent Speaking

Task 1 Store-Bought Presents vs. Homemade Presents   96

Integrated Speaking

Task 2 Moving Student Orientation   100

Task 3 Sociology: Sibling Rivalry   103

Task 4 Animal Science: Earthworms Help Plant Growth   106

Chapter 07

Independent Speaking

Task 1 Students Should Have Part-Time Job Experience   110

Integrated Speaking

Task 2 Fitness Center Renovation   114

Task 3 Business: Giving Samples   117

Task 4 Agriculture: Organic Farming   120

Chapter 08

Independent Speaking

Task 1 Driving Cars vs. Taking Public Transportation   124

Integrated Speaking

Task 2 Spring Concert Series   128

Task 3 Psychology: Mental Accounting   131

Task 4 Animal Science: Electric Fish   134

Part C | Experiencing the TOEFL iBT Actual Tests

Actual Test 01   138

Actual Test 02   146

Appendix | Master Word List

155

How Is This Book Different?

TOEFL® Map Speaking Basic prepares students for success on the TOEFL® iBT with a unique curriculum. Above all, in Part B, students are provided with plenty of activities and exercises. The activities and the exercises for each task are specially designed to develop skills particular to that task. The idea boxes and the note sections will assist students in developing a logical and organized response to each prompt. The guided responses will help students create their own responses, and the sample responses can provide an extra bit of assistance.

The primary emphasis of *TOEFL® Map Speaking Basic* is on developing ideas. In order to be successful on the TOEFL, especially on the independent speaking tasks, students must be able to think quickly and use their ideas to develop complete responses. *TOEFL® Map Speaking Basic* addresses this need with warm-up questions and idea webs. The questions help students generate ideas that can be used to create a response. The idea webs allow students to map out their ideas before planning their responses.

Another unique feature of *TOEFL® Map Speaking Basic* is that its format provides students with the opportunity to gain an in-depth understanding of each question type. The tasks on the TOEFL® iBT Speaking test can be confusing, but *TOEFL® Map Speaking Basic* will give students a deep understanding of each question type. The following unique features of this book, found in Part B, help accomplish that goal.

Warm-up Questions

For the independent speaking tasks, students are presented with three questions related to the prompt. The questions are designed to help students think about the questions in a way that allows them to form opinions and reasons.

Sample Response

Each task in the book includes a sample response that shows students what a high-scoring response looks like. While this response helps students see the aspects of an ideal response, they should understand that a response can include some errors and still receive a high score.

Focusing

Each integrated task ends with a focus on one of the following skills: stress, pronunciation, viewpoints, and paraphrasing. Each skill is extremely useful for performing well on the TOEFL® iBT.

How to Use This Book

The exercises and the questions for each task in *TOEFL® Map Speaking Basic* have been designed to sharpen individual skills. The material found within these pages will gradually prepare students to master the TOEFL® iBT Speaking test. Part C provides two complete sample tests that are modeled on the actual test. Teachers are encouraged to utilize every aspect of the book. Students should follow the directions presented for each task and skip none of the tasks. This method will provide the most benefit to students in terms of both their speaking and test-taking abilities. Before beginning Part B of the book, teachers may wish to review the TOEFL® iBT Speaking scoring rubric with students. That rubric is provided on page 23. This will give students and teachers a more complete understanding of how to respond to each task.

Part A Understanding Speaking Question Types

This section is designed to make students familiar with the types of questions found on the TOEFL® iBT Speaking test. Each question, called a "task," is explained in a simple and clear way. The purpose is to give students an in-depth understanding of each task. Part A also explains the exercises for each task and how to complete them. It is vital that students and teachers review Part A before completing Part B and Part C.

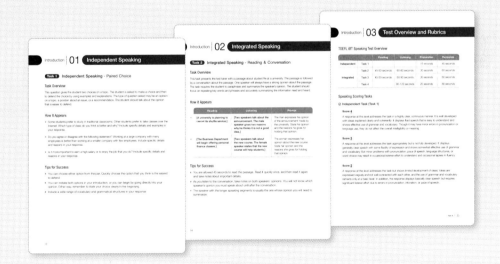

Part B Building Knowledge & Skills for the Speaking Test

Independent Speaking Task 1

The independent tasks are full of activities to help students think critically and to organize their ideas. Students should use the tasks to develop skills that can be used on the test. The specific exercises are as follows:

Warming Up

This exercise helps students respond quickly about personal opinions. Students should respond naturally without worrying about the quality of their answers. The goal is to warm up, not to produce a perfect response.

Brainstorming

The first part of this exercise is the idea box, which includes ideas that students can use in their own responses. Students can use these ideas to complete the idea webs for each task.

Organizing

Students write their brainstorming ideas down in an organized fashion that can be used when giving their responses to the prompt.

Speaking

Students give their responses to the prompt. The guided response can be filled in before answering if students require additional assistance.

Comparing

The high-scoring response lets students hear an example of a response that fulfills all the criteria for a high score. Students should use this response to improve their own scores.

Integrated Speaking Task 2 & 3

In tasks 2 and 3, students are given plenty of exercises to maximize their understanding of the TOEFL® iBT. The exercises are designed not only to promote critical thinking but also to give students the tools they need to master each task. More information on the exercises for tasks 2 and 3 is provided below.

Reading - Analyzing

Students are presented with questions related to the reading passage. The first question helps students paraphrase the key idea or concept in the reading. The second and third questions check reading comprehension.

Listening - Summarizing

Students are asked to briefly paraphrase the information contained in the listening portion of the integrated task.

Synthesizing

Tasks 3 and 4 ask the students to synthesize the information in the reading and listening portions. This exercise is designed to ensure that students have a complete understanding of the information in the task.

Speaking

Students respond to the prompt and can use the guided response if they desire.

Comparing

Students can hear a model response in order to find areas of their own responses that need to be improved.

Focusing

Focusing on Stress in task 2 helps students better understand word stress in spoken English. This is a basic skill that will benefit students in every task. In task 3, Focusing on Pronunciation helps students develop this crucial skill. Pronunciation is important on all parts of the TOEFL® iBT Speaking test. Therefore, this section includes words that many students have difficulty pronouncing correctly.

Integrated Speaking Task 4

The goal of task 4 is to briefly summarize a lecture and then to restate the key points about what the lecturer describes. To meet this goal, *TOEFL® Map Speaking Basic* offers specific exercises to help students quickly prepare strong responses to the prompt.

Listening - Summarizing

While listening to the lecture, students can take notes in the space provided. The notes are partially completed, but students may add more information if they wish. After listening, students are asked to verbally summarize the lecture. This exercise serves as an effective warm-up activity.

Speaking

Students respond to the prompt by using their organized notes for help. A guided response can be completed before responding for students who wish to focus more on pronunciation and delivery.

Comparing

The sample response shows students how to deliver a strong response to the prompt. It can be used to evaluate students' responses.

Focusing

In task 4, Focusing on Paraphrasing emphasizes using various grammar and vocabulary, which is very important in task 4.

Part C Experiencing the TOEFL iBT Actual Tests

This final portion of the book gives students a chance to experience an actual TOEFL® iBT test. There are two sets of tests that are modeled on the speaking section of the TOEFL® iBT. The questions and the topics are similar to those on the real test. Taking these tests allows students the opportunity to measure their own performance ability on an actual test.

Part A

Understanding Speaking Question Types

Introduction 01 | Independent Speaking
Introduction 02 | Integrated Speaking
Introduction 03 | Test Overview and Rubrics

Task 1 - Independent Speaking - Paired Choice

Task Overview

This question gives the student two choices on a topic. The student is asked to make a choice and then to defend the choice by using examples and explanations. The type of question asked may be an opinion on a topic, a position about an issue, or a recommendation. The student should talk about the opinion that is easier to defend.

How It Appears

▶ Some students prefer to study in traditional classrooms. Other students prefer to take classes over the Internet. Which type of class do you think is better and why? Include specific details and examples in your response.

▶ Do you agree or disagree with the following statement? Working at a large company with many employees is better than working at a smaller company with few employees. Include specific details and reasons in your response.

▶ Is it more important to earn a high salary or to enjoy the job that you do? Include specific details and reasons in your response.

Tips for Success

■ You can choose either option from the pair. Quickly choose the option that you think is the easiest to defend.
■ You can restate both options in your introduction, or you can begin by going directly into your opinion. Either way, remember to state your choice clearly in the beginning.
■ Include a wide range of vocabulary and grammatical structures in your response.

Example of the Task

⊘ Question

Some people think that it is okay to eat fast food. Other people think that eating fast food is unhealthy. Which of these two opinions do you agree with? Include specific details and reasons in your response.

01-01

Preparation time: 15 seconds | Response time: 45 seconds

⊘ Sample Response

Introduction Some people believe that eating fast food is fine. But I am convinced that eating any fast food is unhealthy.

Detail 1 For one, fast food is very high in fat and calories. To give an example, one burger meal at a local fast-food restaurant has 1,200 calories and seventy grams of fat. Foods that are so high in fat and calories cannot be healthy.

Detail 2 On top of this, people today do not lead active lifestyles. Most people get very little exercise or none at all. This makes fast food even more dangerous. So it is not surprising that more people are overweight today than ever before.

⊘ Explanation

A four-point response to the first task should clearly defend one side of an issue. In this task, the student is asked to give an opinion about an issue. The sample response begins with a thesis statement that directly states the speaker's opinion ("eating any fast food is unhealthy"). The two supporting details are not mentioned in the introduction. This allows the speaker to give a more detailed response within the given time. The response is broken down into two supporting reasons. The speaker's first reason is that fast food is very high in fat and calories. The speaker then gives an example to explain why. For the second supporting reason ("people today do not lead active lifestyles"), the speaker explains that eating fast food can cause people to become overweight.

Task Overview

This task presents the test taker with a passage about student life at a university. The passage is followed by a conversation about the passage. One speaker will always have a strong opinion about the passage. The task requires the student to paraphrase and summarize the speaker's opinion. The student should focus on repeating key words and phrases and accurately summarizing the information read and heard.

How It Appears

Reading	Listening	Prompt
▶ [A university is planning to cancel its shuttle service.]	[Two speakers talk about the announcement. The male speaker gives two reasons why he thinks it is not a good idea.]	The man expresses his opinion of the announcement made by the university. State his opinion and the reasons he gives for holding that opinion.
▶ [The Business Department will begin offering personal finance classes.]	[Two speakers talk about the new course. The female speaker states that the new course will help students.]	The woman expresses her opinion about the new course. State her opinion and the reasons she gives for holding that opinion.

Tips for Success

- You are allowed 45 seconds to read the passage. Read it quickly once, and then read it again and take notes about important details.

- As you listen to the conversation, take notes on both speakers' opinions. You will not know which speaker's opinion you must speak about until after the conversation.

- The speaker with the longer speaking segments is usually the one whose opinion you will need to summarize.

Example of the Task

⊘ Reading

A university has decided to remove abandoned bicycles from bicycle racks around the campus. Read the announcement from the university. You will have 45 seconds to read the announcement. Begin reading now.

Removing Abandoned Bicycles

This is a notice from the university Maintenance Department. The university has received several complaints from students about abandoned bicycles in the campus bicycle racks. Students have complained that the abandoned bicycles are taking up too much space. In response to these complaints, the university will begin removing the abandoned bicycles immediately. All abandoned bicycles will be sold for scrap. We thank you for your cooperation in this matter.

⊘ Listening

Now listen to two students as they discuss the announcement.

01-02

M: This is just so unfair.

W: What are you talking about?

M: I'm talking about the university's decision to remove abandoned bikes from the bike racks. It's just not the right thing to do.

W: I have to disagree with you. Those abandoned bikes are real eyesores. They are missing their seats and wheels. And some of them don't even have handlebars.

M: Even so, the school can't just throw the bikes away.

W: Sure they can. These abandoned bikes are taking up good parking spaces in the bike racks. When I ride my bike, I have to park really far away. Then, I have to waste time walking to the places I want to go.

M: Well, if the school is going to get rid of the bikes, then the administration needs to give at least two weeks' notice. That way, the owners can get the bikes back if they want.

⊘ Question

The woman gives her opinion about the university's decision. State her opinion and the reasons she gives for holding her opinion.

- -

Preparation time: 30 seconds | Response time: 60 seconds

01-03

⊘ Sample Response

Introduction   The speakers are discussing their school's decision to remove abandoned bicycles from the bike racks. The woman is in favor of the plan. She gives two reasons to support her opinion.

Detail 1   First, she states that the abandoned bikes are real eyesores. She explains that the bikes are missing their seats, tires, and handlebars.

Detail 2   The woman then complains that the abandoned bikes are taking up good parking spaces. She says that students who ride bicycles have to park their bikes far away and waste time walking.

⊘ Explanation

The second task requires the student to understand one speaker's opinion in relation to the reading passage. This requires the student to summarize and paraphrase information from both the reading passage and conversation. The sample response begins by giving a basic summary of the woman's opinion and her reasons for holding it. It then moves on to more detailed explanations. The speaker uses good transitions to move between thoughts. The level of vocabulary is appropriate for the task, and the speaker uses key words and phrases from the passage ("real eyesores" and "taking up good parking spaces"). Overall, the speaker clearly summarizes the woman's opinion and the reasons for her opinion in a well-organized manner.

Task 3 Integrated Speaking - Reading & Lecture

Task Overview

This task focuses on an academic topic. The test takers must first read a short passage that gives general information about the topic. Then, the test taker listens to part of a lecture, which gives details and examples of the topic. The test taker should take notes while listening and then write down the key words and ideas from the lecture. The test taker must be able to summarize the key points from both the reading passage and lecture.

How It Appears

Reading	Listening	Prompt
[Plant Biology – An explanation of how plants survive in the desert]	[The lecture describes two desert plants and how they store water.]	The professor describes two types of desert plants. Describe how these examples explain how plants survive in the desert.
[Advertising – A description of how hidden messages can influence people to buy products]	[The professor talks about an advertisement that used hidden messages and its outcome.]	The professor discusses the use of hidden messages in an advertisement. Describe the advertisement and how it influenced people's buying habits.

Tips for Success

- Take notes on the main idea and any important details while you read.
- The reading passage introduces a general concept. The listening will give more specific examples of the concept from the reading. Be prepared to explain how these examples relate to the information in the reading passage.
- Listen for transition words in the lecture. They will help you organize your notes.

Example of the Task

⊘ Reading

Now read a passage about the observation method. You have 45 seconds to read the passage. Begin reading now.

The Observation Method

An important part of marketing is learning which products customers like to buy. Stores use several methods to gather this information. One of the most common methods they use is the observation method. In the observation method, researchers watch customers while they shop. The researchers take notes on how the customers shop. They also note what products customers buy the most. With this data, stores can make their marketing more effective.

⊘ Listening

Now listen to part of a lecture on this topic in a business class.

Professor (Female)

01-04

Now let's talk about the observation method in action at a grocery store.

One way to get information is to talk directly to customers. Researchers ask customers about their shopping experiences. This way, researchers can get detailed information about individual shoppers. But being direct has some drawbacks. Customers who are asked questions by researchers tend to give false answers. So the direct method can make it difficult to create useful advertising.

Then there's the indirect observation method. This lets a researcher secretly observe customers. So this data tends to be more objective. The researchers simply report facts. For example, they record data such as how many people visit each section of the store. So what's the drawback? This form of observation provides only general information. Still, the indirect method can help stores create more effective marketing campaigns for all their customers.

⊘ Question

The professor talks about two types of observation methods. Explain the observation method and how the examples describe this concept.

01-05

Preparation time: 30 seconds | Response time: 60 seconds

⊘ Sample Response

Introduction   The topic of the reading passage is the observation method in marketing. This is the act of researching how customers shop in order to create more effective marketing. To illustrate this concept, the instructor talks about direct and indirect observation methods.

Detail 1   For the direct method, researchers ask customers about their shopping experiences. This method allows researchers to get detailed information. However, customers do not always give honest answers to researchers.

Detail 2   The indirect method allows researchers to observe customers as they shop. Using this method, marketers can gather objective data about customers' shopping habits.

⊘ Explanation

The goal of the third task is to show that students are able to combine material from written and spoken sources. Student responses must accurately convey important information from both sources. In the sample response, the student first summarizes the concept in the reading passage: the observation method. The student then gives a brief and clear description of the observation method. The speaker moves on to the examples given by the professor. The student first describes the direct method and its benefits and drawbacks. The speaker ends by explaining the indirect method and how it benefits marketers.

Task 4 Integrated Speaking - Lecture

Task Overview

This task involves listening to part of a lecture about an academic topic. The passage does not require students to know anything about the topic beforehand, but it does require an advanced vocabulary. When giving their responses, students should demonstrate that they are able to summarize the key points from the lecture and accurately explain the connection between the general ideas and the concrete examples in the lecture.

How It Appears

Listening	Prompt
▶ [A lecture about how two different animal species hunt together]	Using points and examples from the lecture, explain how hawks and foxes help each other hunt for food.
▶ [An explanation about cultural transmission]	Using points and examples from the lecture, explain how cultural transmission allows people in a society to learn and pass on new information.

Tips for Success

- Listen for words that the professor emphasizes as well as any technical terms and vocabulary. Write them down and include them in your summary.

- Organize your notes into two sections: main idea and details. While listening, circle any words that you feel are key words which you should include in your response.

- The professor will not always give strong signal words to separate ideas. As you listen, take organized notes to establish the lecture's organization.

Example of the Task

⊘ Listening

Now listen to part of a lecture in a sociology class.

Professor (Male)

01-06

So the last time, we said that peer pressure forces people to adopt the values of a group. Today, let's examine how peer pressure can be both positive and negative.

Now, a lot of times, people consider peer pressure to be a bad thing. This is for a good reason. Most young people feel the need to fit in . . . to become more popular . . . with other students at their schools. And research shows that this form of peer pressure—to act cool—often causes problems. It causes students to try risky behavior. For example, they may try dangerous activities such as smoking and drinking alcohol.

But not all peer pressure is bad. A lot of times, peer pressure can actually be beneficial. It can motivate students to improve themselves. Need an example? All right. Let's say a student with average grades has friends who are very motivated to get good grades. The student may start to feel a little jealous or be embarrassed about her lower grades. As you can guess, the student will begin to feel pressure to improve her grades. Otherwise, she may get left out of the group. So peer pressure can result in positive behavior.

⊘ Question

The professor explains the concept of peer pressure. Using points and examples from the lecture, explain how peer pressure can be both negative and positive.

01-07

Preparation time: 20 seconds | Response time: 60 seconds

⊘ Sample Response

Introduction   The professor talks about peer pressure. Peer pressure causes people to follow the behavior of a group. According to the professor, peer pressure can be both negative and positive.

Detail 1   For his first example, the professor talks about negative peer pressure. He explains that when students try to become more popular, they often try dangerous activities. These include smoking and drinking.

Detail 2   On the other hand, peer pressure can be positive. For instance, some students have friends who are very motivated to get good grades. As a result, they feel pressure to get better grades themselves.

⊘ Explanation

The fourth task calls on students to summarize the information in a lecture. Students must be sure to repeat the information as accurately and completely as possible. The sample response briefly summarizes the topic of the lecture and then moves on to explain the two examples that the professor gives. The speaker uses clear and basic transitions ("for his example" and "on the other hand") to move between the two examples. She uses a mixture of grammatical forms and incorporates vocabulary from the lecture ("become more popular" and "very motivated"). While summarizing each example, the speaker explains how the example ties in with the main argument, which is that peer pressure can be both positive and negative.

TOEFL iBT Speaking Test Overview

		Reading	Listening	Preparation	Response
Independent	Task 1			15 seconds	45 seconds
Integrated	Task 2	45-50 seconds	60-80 seconds	30 seconds	60 seconds
	Task 3	45-50 seconds	60-90 seconds	30 seconds	60 seconds
	Task 4		90-120 seconds	20 seconds	60 seconds

Speaking Scoring Tasks

⊘ Independent Task (Task 1)

Score <u>4</u>

A response at this level addresses the task in a highly clear, continuous manner. It is well developed with ideas explained clearly and coherently. It displays fluid speech that is easy to understand and shows effective use of grammar and vocabulary. Though it may have minor errors in pronunciation or language use, they do not affect the overall intelligibility or meaning.

Score <u>3</u>

A response at this level addresses the task appropriately but is not fully developed. It displays generally clear speech with some fluidity of expression and shows somewhat effective use of grammar and vocabulary. But minor problems with pronunciation, pace of speech, language structures, or word choice may result in occasional listener effort to understand and occasional lapses in fluency.

Score <u>2</u>

A response at this level addresses the task but shows limited development of ideas. Ideas are expressed vaguely and not well connected with each other, and the use of grammar and vocabulary remains only at a basic level. In addition, the response displays basically clear speech but requires significant listener effort due to errors in pronunciation, intonation, or pace of speech.

Score 1

A response at this level is very short and practically not related to the task. It lacks substance beyond the expression of very basic ideas and is hard for the listener to understand due to consistent pronunciation, stress, and intonation problems and a severely limited control of grammar and vocabulary.

Score 0

A response at this level is not relevant to the task or has no substance.

⊘ Integrated Tasks (Tasks 2 - 4)

Score 4

A response at this level effectively addresses the task by presenting the necessary information and the appropriate details. It generally shows clear, fluid, sustained speech and effective control of grammar and vocabulary. Though it may have minor errors in pronunciation, intonation, or language use, they do not affect the overall intelligibility or meaning.

Score 3

A response at this level addresses the task appropriately but is not fully developed. It conveys the necessary information but does not include sufficient details. It shows generally clear speech with some fluidity of expression, but minor problems with pronunciation, intonation, or pacing may result in some listener effort. It also displays somewhat effective use of grammar and vocabulary despite the existence of some incorrect word choice or language structures.

Score 2

A response at this level conveys some relevant information, but the ideas are not well connected. It omits key ideas, shows limited development, or exhibits a misunderstanding of key ideas. It shows clear speech occasionally but mostly demonstrates difficulties with pronunciation, intonation, or pace of speech—problems that require significant listener effort. It also displays only a basic level of grammar and vocabulary, which results in the limited or vague expression of ideas or unclear connections.

Score 1

A response at this level is very short and practically not related to the task. It fails to provide much relevant content and contains inaccurate or vague expressions of ideas. It is characterized by fragmented speech with frequent pauses and hesitations and consistent pronunciation and intonation problems. It also shows a severely limited range and control of grammar and vocabulary.

Score 0

A response at this level is not relevant to the task or has no substance.

Part B

Building Knowledge & Skills for the Speaking Test

Chapter 01

Independent Speaking

Task 1   Children Should Receive Money for Chores

Integrated Speaking

Task 2   Library to Reduce Book Collection

Task 3   Statistics: Sampling Bias

Task 4   Plant Biology: Trees Shedding Leaves

Task 1 Children Should Receive Money for Chores

Warming Up >> Choose a question at random from the list below. Answer the question right away without making notes. Try to speak for at least 10 seconds.

- What kinds of chores do you usually do? *I usually clean my room and take out the garbage.*
- How can paying children to do chores motivate them to work harder?
- Why do you think some parents do not pay their children for doing chores?

? Question

Do you agree or disagree with the following statement? Children should receive money for doing household chores. Include specific details and reasons in your response.

Brainstorming

Choose one of the two opinions you want to speak about. Then, read over the phrases below. Decide which phrases can be used to support your opinion. Finally, choose the correct words to fill out the idea web.

___
Choice 1 Receive Money

▶ Word List

- money is a reason to work hard
- encourages children to work well
- learn that work is rewarded with money
- important concept in life
- also teaches about rewards
- children do not like doing chores

▶ Idea Web

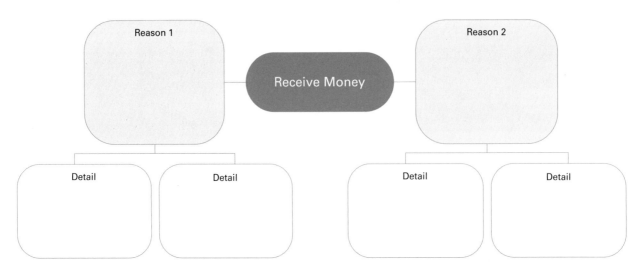

Choice 2 Not Receive Money

▶ Word List

- family must work together
- paying for chores is also unequal
- parents get no pay for chores
- children should not get special treatment
- learn about responsibility
- everybody should help out

▶ Idea Web

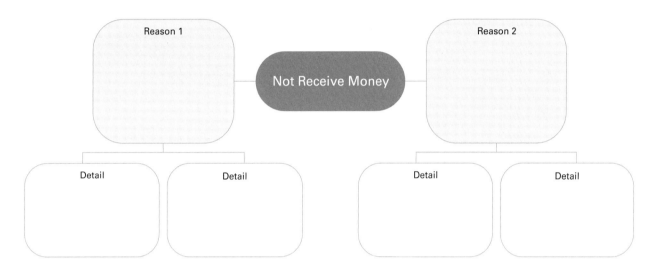

Reason 1

Not Receive Money

Reason 2

Detail Detail Detail Detail

Organizing

Look back at the idea web. Use it to organize your response.

My Choice *Receive Money / Not Receive Money*

First Reason

Details

Second Reason

Details

Speaking

Now give your spoken response for 45 seconds. You may use the guided response to assist you.

Guided Response 1 Receive Money

I agree that children should _____ for doing household chores. For one, giving

money to children for doing chores can _____ them to work hard. Not many

children like _____. So paying children gives them a reason to _____

_____ all their tasks. Children can also learn about the idea of _____.

Children learn that doing work allows them to _____. This is a very

_____ in life, so it is important to teach children about it early.

Guided Response 2 Not Receive Money

To me, parents should not have to _____ their children money for doing

chores. First of all, children must learn that chores are a _____. They need

to understand that members of a family all _____ to care for their home.

What's more, paying children for chores is _____. Parents do chores around

the home but do not receive _____. Therefore, children should not receive

_____ when it comes to doing chores.

Comparing Listen to a sample response. Then, compare the response with yours.

Receive Money

02-01

Not Receive Money

02-02

Related Topics

Read the following questions related to the topic. For questions 1 to 3, use the information provided to make responses. For questions 4 and 5, use your own ideas to make responses.

1 All children should do household chores.

Agree	Disagree
- learn skills important for the future - can help their parents	- children should not work - children should play or do homework

2 When you do chores, do you prefer to do indoor or outdoor chores?

Indoor Chores	Outdoor Chores
- enjoy cleaning rooms and doing laundry - too hot to go outside many days	- enjoy spending time outdoors - have fun cutting the grass and doing yardwork

3 When do you prefer to do household chores, in the morning before school or work or after coming home?

In the Morning	After Coming Home
- like to get them out of the way - have free time in the morning but none in the evening	- take a break from doing homework - don't have many → easy to do them at night

4 Some parents make their children do too many household chores.

Agree	Disagree

5 Children should not have to do more than one hour of chores each day.

Agree	Disagree

Task 2 Library to Reduce Book Collection

 **Vocabulary** Take a few moments to review the vocabulary items that will appear in this task.

- **reduce** *v.* to make lower in number
- **upcoming** *adj.* happening in the near future
- **shelf** *n.* a flat, rectangular structure made of wood or metal and used to hold objects
- **section** *n.* one of several parts; a piece
- **exam** *n.* a test

- **period** *n.* a specific length of time during which an event takes place
- **get rid of** *exp.* to do away with; to remove
- **research** *n.* the gathering of information; study
- **waste** *v.* to use carelessly
- **prefer** *v.* to like one thing more than another

Reading

Read the following announcement from a university library.

Library to Reduce the Number of Books

During the upcoming school year, the library is going to reduce the size of its book collection. Thousands of the library's books sit on the shelves without ever being used. Therefore, we will make the book section smaller. This will allow us to make the student computer center larger. As a result, more students will be able to use the computers in the library during exam periods.

Analyzing Choose the best answer for each question below.

1   What is the purpose of the announcement?
    Ⓐ To request more computers for the library
    Ⓑ To inform students about a change at the university
    Ⓒ To encourage students to read more books

2   Why does the announcement mention the bookshelves?
    Ⓐ To explain the cost of buying library books
    Ⓑ To illustrate the size of the library's problem
    Ⓒ To request more books for the library

3   What will the school do with the space created by the plan?
    Ⓐ Buy more computers to give to students
    Ⓑ Create a study area during exam periods
    Ⓒ Increase the size of the computer center

Listening

Listen to a short conversation related to the reading. Take notes about the woman's opinion.

Summarizing Use the chart below to explain the woman's opinion about the announcement.

Main Idea The woman feels that the university's plan is a _____ .

Reason 1 She believes that the books are _____ in the library. The space could be used to make new _____ for students.

Reason 2 She also mentions that most students _____ doing their research online. By making the computer center _____ , more students will be able to do their _____ during busy times.

Synthesizing

Give a brief spoken response to the questions based on the announcement and the conversation.

1 What is the man's reaction to the announcement?

   → *The man feels that the plan* _____ .

2 Why is the woman's reaction to the announcement?

   → *The woman feels differently than the man by saying that the plan is a* _____ .

3 How can students benefit from the plan?

   → *Students can benefit because the computer center* _____ .

◀ Speaking

Now give your spoken response for 60 seconds. You may use the guided response to assist you.

? Question

The woman expresses her opinion about the university's plan. Explain her opinion and the reasons she gives for holding it.

Guided Response

The man and the woman are talking about the university's plans to get rid of _____.

The woman _____ with the plan. She explains that the books not used by

students simply _____ in the library. She feels that the library could use this

space to create new _____ for students. The woman also mentions that most

students choose to do their research _____. Furthermore, the woman believes

that more students will be able to do their schoolwork during _____ if the

computer lab is _____.

Comparing Listen to a sample response. Then, compare the response with yours.

02-04

⊙FOCUSING ON STRESS Read the following sentences. Be sure to stress the parts in bold.

✓ Dur**ing** the **up**coming **school year**, the **li**bra**ry** is go**ing to** re**duce** the **size** of its **book co**llection.

✓ Get**ting rid** of the **books** that **no**body ever **uses** is a **smart move**.

✓ **She** be**lieves** that the **books** are was**ting space** in the **li**bra**ry**.

Task 3 Statistics: Sampling Bias

◎ Vocabulary Take a few moments to review the vocabulary items that will appear in this task.

- **survey** *n.* a collection of opinions that represents the opinions of many
- **gather** *v.* to bring things together into a group; to collect
- **include** *v.* to put in a group; to contain
- **method** *n.* a way of completing a job
- **produce** *v.* to bring forth; to develop

- **election** *n.* the act of choosing a leader
- **vote** *v.* to decide on a leader
- **headline** *n.* the title of a newspaper article
- **conduct** *v.* to carry out; to control
- **margin** *n.* an extra amount

▌ Reading

Read the following passage about sampling bias.

Sampling Bias

Statistical surveys are an important way to gather information about large groups of people. However, some surveys do not include all of the members of a group. When this happens, it is called sampling bias. Sampling bias often occurs because a small number of survey methods are used. The main problem with sampling bias is that it often produces results that are incorrect.

Analyzing Choose the best answer for each question below.

1 What is the main idea of the passage?
- Ⓐ Sampling bias creates problems for many people.
- Ⓑ Surveys are the best way to get information about people.
- Ⓒ Sampling bias can create inaccurate survey results.

2 How are sampling biased surveys different from regular surveys?
- Ⓐ They produce more accurate results.
- Ⓑ They fail to include all of the members of a group.
- Ⓒ They are better for large groups of people.

3 What causes sampling bias to occur?
- Ⓐ Giving surveys to large numbers of people
- Ⓑ Using only a few survey methods
- Ⓒ Including all members of a group in a survey

Listening

Listen to a short lecture related to the reading. Take notes on key words and specific information from the lecture.

> **Notes**
>
> Topic   *1948 presidential*
>
> Detail 1   *newspaper story: Dewey*
>
>   *headline made from*
>
> Detail 2   *only rich people had*
>
>   *survey results*
>
> Key Words   *before votes were counted;*

Summarizing Use the chart below to explain the main idea and the key points of the lecture.

Topic   The main idea of the lecture is the _____.

Detail 1 The professor explains that one newspaper incorrectly wrote that Dewey _____ in the election. The newspaper wrote this story based on a _____.

Detail 2 The survey was done _____, so it only included rich people. These people were more likely to _____. Therefore, the survey results were _____.

Synthesizing

Give a brief spoken response to the questions based on the reading passage and the lecture.

1   What is the main problem with sampling bias?

   → *The main problem with sampling bias is that it produces* _____.

2   What was the survey method talked about in the lecture?

   → *The survey method talked about in the lecture was* _____.

3   How did this survey method affect the results of the survey?

   → *This method affected the results by including only* _____.

Speaking

Now give your spoken response for 60 seconds. You may use the guided response to assist you.

? Question

The professor explains sampling bias by giving one example. Explain the example and how it explains the concept of sampling bias.

Guided Response

The topic of the reading passage is _____ . This is when a survey does not

include _____ of a group. It usually creates _____ .

To explain sampling bias, the professor talks about the 1948 _____ . He

explains that one newspaper said that Thomas Dewey _____ President Truman

in the election. This _____ was based on a survey. The survey was done

_____ , so only _____ were included. Consequently,

the result of the survey was _____ .

Comparing Listen to a sample response. Then, compare the response with yours.

02-06

⊙FOCUSING ON PRONUNCIATION Practice saying these words by using natural intonation.

survey	information	method	election	telephone
✓	✓	✓	✓	✓

Task 4 Plant Biology: Trees Shedding Leaves

🎯 Vocabulary   Take a few moments to review the vocabulary items that will appear in this task.

- **shed** v. to fall off; to drop out
- **protect** v. to keep from being damaged or injured; to defend
- **moisture** n. wetness
- **trunk** n. the main part of a tree

- **branch** n. a part of a tree that grows out of the trunk
- **survive** v. to live
- **layer** n. one thickness of something over another
- **root** n. the part of a plant that is underground

◀ Listening

Listen to a lecture on the topic of trees shedding their leaves. Take notes on key words and concepts in the lecture.

> **Notes**
>
> Topic   *trees shedding leaves; done to _____ themselves*
>
> Detail 1   *live in cold climates; leaves use a lot of _____*
>
> *keeping leaves alive causes trees to lose _____*
>
> Detail 2   *leaves start to die; fall to the _____*
>
> *forms a protective _____*
>
> Key Words *cold climates; air becomes dry; _____*

02-07

Summarizing   Using your own words, summarize the topic of the lecture, describe how the professor explains the topic, and restate the key points.

Topic   In the lecture, the professor explains why trees _____. She claims that trees do this to protect themselves.

Detail 1   During the winter, the leaves need a lot of _____. If the trees give moisture to the leaves, they might _____. So they keep moisture inside their trunks and _____.

Detail 2   The leaves die and fall _____. This creates a _____ that protects the roots of the trees.

Speaking

Now give your spoken response for 60 seconds. You may use the guided response to assist you.

? Question

Using points and examples from the talk, explain why trees shed their leaves.

Guided Response

The lecture mainly discusses why trees _____ during winter. According to the speaker, trees do this to _____ . During the winter, trees use a lot of _____ to keep their leaves alive. If the trees lose too much moisture, they can _____ . So they keep their moisture inside their trunks and _____ . This causes _____ to die. As they fall to the ground, they form a _____ over the roots of the trees. Together, these factors allow the trees to live _____ .

Comparing Listen to a sample response. Then, compare the response with yours.

02-08

☀FOCUSING ON PARAPHRASING Read the follow sentences and their paraphrased sentences. Then, practice saying each sentence with natural intonation.

✓ The lecture mainly discusses why trees lose their leaves during winter.

→ The purpose of the talk is to explain why leaves fall off trees.

✓ During the winter, trees use a lot of moisture to keep their leaves alive.

→ Trees need to give their leaves a lot of water to keep them alive during the winter.

✓ As they fall to the ground, they form a protective layer over the roots of the trees.

→ The leaves on the ground cover the roots, helping to protect them.

Part B

Chapter 02

Independent Speaking

Task 1   Deciding on a Teacher to Hire

Integrated Speaking

Task 2   University Housing Policy Change

Task 3   Business: Promotions

Task 4   Animal Science: Display Behavior

Task 1 Deciding on a Teacher to Hire

Warming Up ≫ Choose a question at random from the list below. Answer the question right away without making notes. Try to speak for at least 10 seconds.

- What are some advantages of learning arts and crafts? *I can learn to work with my hands. I can also become more creative by doing arts and crafts.*
- What is the importance of computer programming nowadays?
- How important is it for young people to be in good shape?

? Question

A school has extra money in its budget, so it is planning to hire a new teacher. Which of the following teachers should the school hire?

- An arts and crafts teacher
- A computer programming teacher
- A physical education teacher

Use details and examples to explain your answer.

Brainstorming

Choose one of the three choices you want to speak about. Then, read over the phrases below. Decide which phrases can be used to support your opinion. Finally, choose the correct words to fill out the idea web.

Choice 1 Hire an Arts and Crafts Teacher

▶ **Word List**

- become more creative
- classes not always interesting
- be proud of their new ideas
- come up with unique designs
- enjoy making things during class
- can do fun activities

▶ **Idea Web**

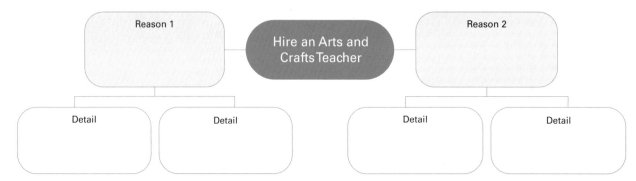

<u>Choice 2</u> **Hire a Computer Programming Teacher**

▶ **Word List**

- understand computers better
- computers important in society
- get valuable experience

- jobs require programming skills
- use to work, play, and study
- help get a job in the future

▶ **Idea Web**

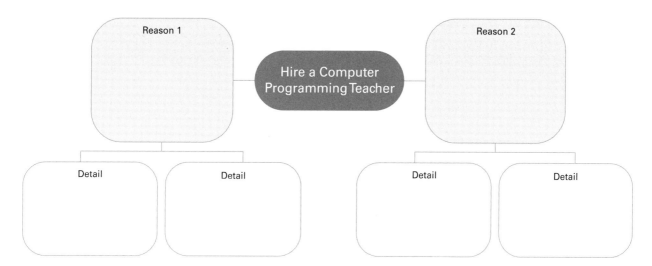

Organizing

Look back at the idea web. Use it to organize your response.

My Choice *Hire an Arts and Crafts Teacher / Hire a Computer Programming Teacher*

First Reason

Details

Second Reason

Details

● Speaking

Now give your spoken response for 45 seconds. You may use the guided response to assist you.

Guided Response 1 **Hire an Arts and Crafts Teacher**

In my opinion, the school _____ hire an arts and crafts teacher. First, arts

and crafts are _____ activities for students. Many school classes are pretty

_____ for students. But they will have _____ of fun

making things during their arts and crafts classes. In addition, the teacher can help the students become

_____ . For instance, they can think of _____ to make.

After making things, they will be proud since it will show their _____ .

Guided Response 2 **Hire a Computer Programming Teacher**

Of the three choices, the best one is to _____ a computer programming

teacher. To begin with, computers are an extremely important part of _____

now. People use computers to work, _____ , and study. A computer

programming teacher can _____ students in understanding computers better.

Secondly, many jobs require workers to have computer programming _____ .

If students learn programming, they can get _____ experience. That will help

them get good jobs that pay lots of _____ after graduation.

Comparing Listen to a sample response. Then, compare the response with yours.

Hire an Arts and
Crafts Teacher

Hire a Computer
Programming Teacher

02-09

02-10

Related Topics

Read the following questions related to the topic. For questions 1 to 3, use the information provided to make responses. For questions 4 and 5, use your own ideas to make responses.

1   Schools should not teach art and music classes.

Agree	Disagree
- materials for classes are too expensive - are other more important subjects to learn	- fun classes for students - art and music can be inspiring

2   Students should have to take a basic economics class before they graduate.

Agree	Disagree
- can prepare for the future - help learn real-life skills	- can learn from parents - is too advanced should be taught at college

3   Where do you think students should learn to cook, at school or at home?

At School	At Home
- good facilities for cooking - easy for teachers to provide basic instruction	- many parents are good cooks - cooking isn't an academic subject

4   Schools need to spend more money to improve their facilities.

Agree	Disagree

5   When a school expands, should it add a gymnasium or a library?

A Gymnasium	A Library

Task 2 University Housing Policy Change

🎯 Vocabulary Take a few moments to review the vocabulary items that will appear in this task.

- **policy** *n.* a set of rules or ideas about how to do something

- **income** *n.* money that is earned from work or business

- **required** *adj.* needed; essential

- **incoming** *adj.* arriving at or coming to a place

- **dormitory** *n.* a building on a school campus where students can live

- **provide** *v.* to make something available; to give

- **cooperation** *n.* the act of working together to do something

- **financial** *adj.* related to money

- **serious** *adj.* having an important or dangerous result

- **enroll** *v.* to enter as a member or participant

Reading

Read the following announcement from a university.

Housing Policy Change for All Incoming Freshmen

State University students:

Over the past school year, several juniors and seniors have moved out of on-campus housing. This has greatly reduced the school's income. To make up for this, all incoming freshmen will be required to live in the dormitories. The university will provide freshmen with special services. These include free use of laundry machines, participation in study groups, and membership on sports teams. Thank you for your cooperation in this matter.

Sincerely,

Dr. Patricia Levine, President

Analyzing Choose the best answer for each question below.

1   What is the purpose of the announcement?

   Ⓐ To explain a new policy for incoming students

   Ⓑ To encourage students to join study groups and sports teams

   Ⓒ To inform students about new dormitories for freshmen

2   What is the main problem described in the announcement?

   Ⓐ Too many juniors and seniors are living in the dormitories.

   Ⓑ Freshmen want more special services.

   Ⓒ Not enough older students are staying on campus.

3   Which of the following is true according to the announcement?

   Ⓐ All students will receive free laundry service.

   Ⓑ The university is not making enough money.

   Ⓒ Many older students want to live in on-campus housing.

Listening

Listen to a short conversation related to the reading. Take notes about the man's opinion.

> **Notes**
>
> The man (agrees / disagrees) with the announcement.
>
> Reason *incoming students may not want to live in dorms; may not enroll* ....
>
> 02-11
>
> Key Words and Details *financial problems;* ....

Summarizing Use the chart below to explain the man's opinion about the announcement.

Main Idea In the man's opinion, the school's plan may not be the .... to solve the problem.

Reason 1 He worries that not all of the .... will want to live in the dorms. Therefore, they might not .... at the university. If that happens, then the school will not make ....

Reason 2 The man also feels that housing fees are .... By making the dorms ...., more students will .... in them.

Synthesizing

Give a brief spoken response to the questions based on the announcement and the conversation.

1   What is the man's reaction to the announcement?

→ *The man disagrees with the woman. He is not sure that the plan* ....

2   Why does the university want all freshmen to live in the dormitories?

→ *The university wants freshmen to live in the dorms in order to make up for the school's* ....

3   Why does the man think this plan will fail?

→ *He feels this way because many incoming students will not want to* ....

● Speaking

Now give your spoken response for 60 seconds. You may use the guided response to assist you.

? Question

The man expresses his opinion about the announcement. Explain his opinion and the reasons he gives for holding it.

Guided Response

The speakers are discussing the university's _____ change. The woman thinks

the plan is a good idea. However, the man is _____ it will work. His first concern

is that many incoming students will not want to live in the _____ . So they will

not enroll in the university. If this happens, then the university's plan will _____ .

Therefore, the man thinks that the school should make the dorms _____ . Then,

more students will choose to _____ in them.

Comparing Listen to a sample response. Then, compare the response with yours.

02-12

⊛**FOCUSING ON STRESS** Read the following sentences. Be sure to stress the parts in bold.

✓ **All in**com**ing fresh**men will be re**quired** to **live** in the **dor**mi**tor**ies.

✓ The **school's plan** may **not** be the **best way** to **solve** the **prob**lem.

✓ The **man** also **feels** the **dorms** are **too** ex**pen**sive.

Task 3 Business: Promotions

⊚ Vocabulary Take a few moments to review the vocabulary items that will appear in this task.

- **a great deal** *exp.* very many; several
- **influence** *v.* to change something in an indirect way
- **habit** *n.* a usual way of behaving
- **effective** *adj.* producing a result that is wanted
- **campaign** *n.* a series of activities designed to produce a specific result

- **attract** *v.* to catch the attention of someone
- **shape** *v.* to affect the development of
- **particular** *adj.* specific; exact
- **strategy** *n.* a plan used to achieve a goal
- **come up with** *phr v.* to think of something

Reading

Read the following passage about promotions.

Promotions

Nearly all businesses spend a great deal of time and money to influence the buying habits of their customers. One of the most effective ways a business can do this is through promotions. Several types of promotions are common. These include advertising campaigns, special discounts, and product placement. The desired result of promotions is to attract more customers. This, in turn, helps businesses generate more income.

Analyzing Choose the best answer for each question below.

1   What is the purpose of the passage?
  Ⓐ To explain a method businesses use to control customers' buying habits
  Ⓑ To provide advice to businesses on how to generate more income
  Ⓒ To introduce the most common types of promotions

2   What outcome do promotions have for businesses?
  Ⓐ They sometimes decrease businesses' incomes.
  Ⓑ They bring in additional customers.
  Ⓒ They are an effective way to do business.

3   Which of the following examples of promotion are listed in the passage?
  Ⓐ Special discounts, advertising campaigns, and product placement
  Ⓑ Product placement, membership clubs, and customers interviews
  Ⓒ Free gift cards, business sponsorships, and special discounts

Listening

Listen to a short lecture related to the reading. Take notes on key words and specific information from the lecture.

Notes

Topic	*business*
Detail 1	*friend owns restaurant; successful; many customers during dinner*
	but no customers
Detail 2	*came up with a*
	attracted many
Key Words	*promotions essential for success;*

02-13

Summarizing Use the chart below to explain the main idea and the key points of the lecture.

Topic The main topic of the discussion is _____ .

Detail 1 The lecturer first talks about a friend who _____ . His friend always has a lot of customers _____ . However, the friend did not have many customers _____ .

Detail 2 To solve this problem, the friend created a _____ . This _____ many customers to the restaurant before dinnertime. In this way, businesses can _____ more customers and make _____ .

Synthesizing

Give a brief spoken response to the questions based on the reading passage and the lecture.

1 How do promotions help businesses make more money?

→ *Promotions help businesses make more money by* _____ .

2 What type of promotion was described by the lecturer?

→ *He talked about an early-bird special, which is a* _____ .

3 What was the result of the promotion discussed in the lecture?

→ *The promotion discussed in the lecture attracted* _____ *to the restaurant before dinnertime.*

Speaking

Now give your spoken response for 60 seconds. You may use the guided response to assist you.

? Question

The professor explains business promotions by giving one example. Describe the example and how it explains the concept of business promotions.

Guided Response

The reading passage states that businesses use promotions to attract more customers and to

generate _____ . The lecturer explains this idea by mentioning his friend's

_____ . The restaurant always has _____ during

dinnertime. However, it did not have many customers _____ . To solve this

problem, the lecturer's friend created an early-bird _____ promotion. The

plan attracted many customers to the restaurant _____ dinnertime. So

the promotion was a _____ . This example shows how promotions can

_____ more customers and make _____ .

Comparing Listen to a sample response. Then, compare the response with yours.

02-14

FOCUSING ON PRONUNCIATION Practice saying these words by using natural intonation.

promotion	influence	campaign	essential	successful
✓	✓	✓	✓	✓

Task 4 Animal Science: Display Behavior

🎯 Vocabulary   Take a few moments to review the vocabulary items that will appear in this task.

- **interact** v. to talk or do things with others
- **species** n. a group of animals that are similar
- **yell** v. to say something very loudly
- **gain** v. to get something that one wants
- **advantage** n. something that helps make another thing better

- **plumage** n. feathers that cover the body of a bird
- **purpose** n. the reason why something is done or used
- **mating season** n. the time of year when animals produce young
- **central** adj. main; most important

◀ Listening

Listen to a lecture on the topic of display behavior. Take notes on key words and concepts in the lecture.

> **Notes**
>
> Topic   *animals use display behavior to interact with* _____ *of their species*
>
> Detail 1   *monkeys yell at other monkeys; do this to gain* _____
>
> _____ *give*
>
> Detail 2   *male peacocks have plumage; use this to* _____
>
> *show off plumage during* _____
>
> Key Words   *display behavior; monkeys yell; gain advantages;*

02-15

Summarizing   Using your own words, summarize the topic of the lecture, describe how the professor explains the topic, and restate the key points.

Topic   The instructor discusses _____. She illustrates this by talking about _____ and _____.

Detail 1 Monkeys _____ at one another as display behavior. If one monkey finds food, another monkey will give out a _____. This yell _____ the first monkey away from the food.

Detail 2 Male peacocks have _____. The purpose of it is to _____. Male peacocks show off their plumage during _____. Those with the _____ attract the most females.

Speaking

Now give your spoken response for 60 seconds. You may use the guided response to assist you.

? Question

Using points and examples from the lecture, explain display behavior.

Guided Response

In the lecture, the instructor talks about the _____ of animals. She

_____ this by mentioning the display behavior of monkeys and peacocks. First,

the instructor claims that monkeys _____ at one another as a form of display

behavior. If one monkey gets food, another monkey will give a _____ .

This scares the first monkey _____ from the food. The instructor then

talks about the plumage of _____ . She explains that male peacocks use

their _____ to attract females. Those with the best plumage attract the

_____ .

Comparing Listen to a sample response. Then, compare the response with yours.

02-16

FOCUSING ON PARAPHRASING Read the follow sentences and their paraphrased sentences. Then, practice saying each sentence with natural intonation.

✓ She illustrates this by mentioning the display behavior of monkeys and peacocks.

→ The instructor talks about monkeys and peacocks to describe display behavior.

✓ If one monkey gets food, another monkey will give a warning yell.

→ A monkey will produce a warning yell to scare other monkeys away from food.

✓ She explains that male peacocks use their plumage to attract females.

→ According to the instructor, male peacocks use their beautiful feathers to get the attention of females.

Part B

Chapter 03

Independent Speaking
Task 1 Taking Notes in Class vs. Concentrating on Lectures

Integrated Speaking
Task 2 Loaning Laptops to Students
Task 3 Education: Teaching Students to Follow the Rules
Task 4 History: The American Industrial Revolution

Task 1 Taking Notes in Class vs. Concentrating on Lectures

Warming Up >> Choose a question at random from the list below. Answer the question right away without making notes. Try to speak for at least 10 seconds.

- How do you usually study for your classes? *I usually review my notes and read the textbook.*

- What will the teacher think if you sit in class without taking notes?

- In what ways can taking notes make it harder to concentrate?

? Question

Some students like to take notes during class while other students prefer to concentrate on lectures. Which do you think is better and why? Include details in your explanation.

Brainstorming

Choose one of the two opinions you want to speak about. Then, read over the phrases below. Decide which phrases can be used to support your opinion. Finally, choose the correct words to fill out the idea web.

Choice 1 **Taking Notes**

▶ **Word List**

- many classes have participation grades
- lets teacher know I am paying attention
- easily review class material
- teacher thinks do not care about class
- make it easier to study
- cannot remember the entire lecture

▶ **Idea Web**

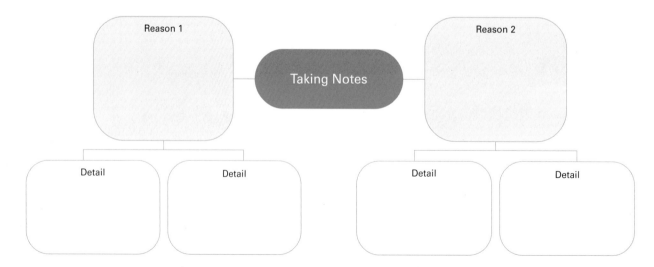

Choice 2 **Concentrating on Lectures**

▶ **Word List**

- share my own ideas in class
- participate more easily as well
- think about the lecture
- ask the teacher questions
- can focus on the material
- taking notes distracting

▶ **Idea Web**

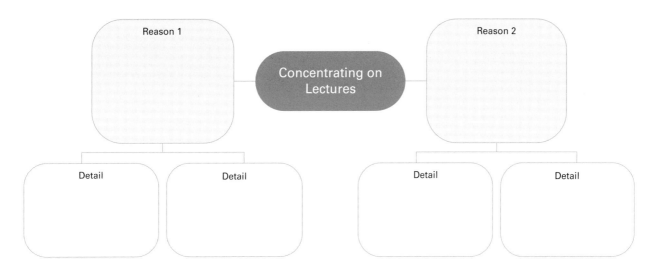

Reason 1

Concentrating on Lectures

Reason 2

Detail Detail Detail Detail

Organizing

Look back at the idea web. Use it to organize your response.

My Choice *Taking Notes / Concentrating on Lectures*

First Reason

Details

Second Reason

Details

Speaking

Now give your spoken response for 45 seconds. You may use the guided response to assist you.

Guided Response 1 Taking Notes

I prefer _____ in class rather than just concentrating on the lectures. To begin with, notes make it _____ . I can easily look at my notes to _____ the material covered in my classes. After all, it's almost impossible to remember _____ of a lecture. Furthermore, taking notes shows the teacher that I'm _____ . This is especially important because many classes have _____ . If I sit in class without taking notes, the teacher will think I _____ about the class.

Guided Response 2 Concentrating on Lectures

Most students take notes in class. As for me, I am convinced that _____ on lectures is better. One reason is that I _____ on the material. When I take notes, I get _____ . By focusing only on lectures, I _____ the material better. Concentrating on lectures also allows me to _____ more easily. I can _____ the lectures and _____ the teacher questions. This way, I can remember the material _____ , so I don't have to study as much outside class.

Comparing Listen to a sample response. Then, compare the response with yours.

Taking Notes

Concentrating on Lectures

02-17

02-18

Related Topics

Read the following questions related to the topic. For questions 1 to 3, use the information provided to make responses. For questions 4 and 5, use your own ideas to make responses.

1 Teachers should not allow students to interrupt class with questions.

Agree	Disagree
- questions can disturb other students	- can help students understand material
- can ask questions after class	- should be interaction between teacher and students

2 When you take a class, do you prefer one where only the teacher speaks or one where there are class discussions?

Only the Teacher Speaks	Class Discussions
- want to learn as much as possible	- lets students show what they know
- student comments rarely contribute anything	- helps students understand material better

3 Students at elementary schools take too many classes.

Agree	Disagree
- can't remember everything they learn	- need to push students to make them learn more
- too tired from studying too much	- 5 or 6 classes a day isn't too many

4 Do you prefer classes that have no homework or a lot of homework?

No Homework	A Lot of Homework

5 Schools should teach more math and science classes and fewer English and history classes.

Agree	Disagree

Task 2 Loaning Laptops to Students

⊚ Vocabulary Take a few moments to review the vocabulary items that will appear in this task.

- **crowded** *adj.* filled with people or objects
- **flexibility** *n.* the ability to change easily
- **employee** *n.* a worker
- **convinced** *adj.* completely sure about something

- **purchase** *v.* to buy
- **assignment** *n.* a job someone has to do
- **run** *v.* to operate; to use something
- **deteriorate** *v.* to become worse
- **check out** *phr v.* to borrow something

◀ Reading

Read the following announcement about a campus situation.

Laptop Loaning Service for Students

Effective the first week of March, the school will begin loaning laptops to students. By providing this service, the university hopes to make the computer labs less crowded. The service will also give students greater flexibility regarding where they choose to study. To borrow a laptop, visit any university computer lab and show your student ID card to a computer center employee.

Analyzing Choose the best answer for each question below.

1   What is the purpose of the announcement?
- Ⓐ To inform students about a new service on campus
- Ⓑ To remind students to bring their ID cards to the computer labs
- Ⓒ To promote a new computer center on campus

2   Which reason is NOT given for letting students borrow laptops?
- Ⓐ Making the computer labs less crowded
- Ⓑ Allowing students to study in different places
- Ⓒ Encouraging students to use computers more often

3   What must students do to borrow a laptop?
- Ⓐ They have to become a member of one of the computer labs on campus.
- Ⓑ They need to show their identification to a worker at a computer lab.
- Ⓒ They must choose where they want to study before checking out a laptop.

Listening

Listen to a short conversation related to the reading. Take notes about the man's opinion.

> **Notes**
>
> The man (agrees / disagrees) with the school's decision.
>
> **Reason** *school needs to purchase new computers for labs; woman could not do*
>
> **Key Words and Details** *most computers really old;*

02-19

Summarizing Use the chart below to explain the man's opinion about the announcement.

Main Idea The man in the conversation is _____ that his school's plan to loan laptops to students will be successful.

Reason 1 For his first argument, the man states that the school needs to buy _____ for the computer labs. He says that most of the computers in the labs are _____ .

Reason 2 The man also worries that the service in the computer labs will _____ . He feels the employees will be _____ to answer questions or to help students with computer problems.

Synthesizing

Give a brief spoken response to the questions based on the announcement and the conversation.

1   What does the university hope to do by loaning laptops to students?

→ *The university hopes to* _____ .

2   What does the man say about the computers in the computer labs?

→ *He says that the computers are* _____ .

3   What does the man say about the workers at the computer labs?

→ *The man says that the workers will be too busy checking out laptops to* _____ _____ .

◗ Speaking

Now give your spoken response for 60 seconds. You may use the guided response to assist you.

? Question

The man expresses his opinion about the school's announcement. Explain his opinion and the reasons he gives for holding it.

Guided Response

The speakers are discussing their school's decision to allow students to _____ .

The man is _____ the plan will work. The man gives _____

to explain his opinion. His first argument is that the computers in the labs are _____ .

The man believes the school should buy _____ instead of laptops. He is also

worried that the service in the computer labs will _____ . He thinks the staff will

be too busy renting laptops to _____ using the labs.

Comparing Listen to a sample response. Then, compare the response with yours.

02-20

⟨⟩ FOCUSING ON STRESS Read the following sentences. Be sure to stress the parts in bold.

✓ The **ser**vice will al**so give** stu**dents great**er **flexibil**ity in **where** they **choose** to **stu**dy.

✓ How**ever**, the **man** is **not** con**vinced** it will **be success**ful.

✓ **He says most** of the com**pu**ters in the **labs** are **really old**.

Task 3 Education: Teaching Students to Follow the Rules

◎ Vocabulary Take a few moments to review the vocabulary items that will appear in this task.

- **lesson** *n.* something learned
- **respect** *v.* to act politely toward others
- **rely on** *phr v.* to need something
- **variety** *n.* a number of different things
- **experience** *n.* something that has happened to a person

- **especially** *adv.* particularly; very
- **exist** *v.* to be real
- **purpose** *n.* a reason
- **create** *v.* to make something

◀▌ Reading

Read the following passage about teaching rules.

Teaching Rules

One of the most important lessons students learn at school is how to follow the rules. Students learn how to share, to respect others, and to complete assignments on time. However, teaching students these ideas is sometimes difficult. As a result, teachers have to rely on a variety of strategies to help students learn to follow the rules.

Analyzing Choose the best answer for each question below.

1   What is the main idea of the passage?
  Ⓐ The most important life lessons are taught in school.
  Ⓑ Learning to follow the rules is important for students.
  Ⓒ It is sometimes difficult to teach students new ideas.

2   What do students learn by following the rules?
  Ⓐ How to use different strategies
  Ⓑ How to share difficult ideas
  Ⓒ How to respect other people

3   Which of the following is true according to the passage?
  Ⓐ School teaches students to finish their work according to a schedule.
  Ⓑ Teaching students to follow the rules is simple to do.
  Ⓒ Students must use a variety of strategies to follow the rules.

Listening

Listen to a short lecture related to the reading. Take notes on key words and specific information from the lecture.

Notes

Topic	*teaching students to*
Detail 1	*young students need to know why a rule exists; otherwise will not*
	teachers must explain
Detail 2	*teacher did not want students eating in class; students did not follow rule*
	after explaining why made rule, students
Key Words	*experience as elementary school teacher;*

02-21

Summarizing Use the chart below to explain the main idea and the key points of the lecture.

Topic The lecturer explains how she taught her elementary students to _____ .

Detail 1 First, she explains that young children love to _____ . She says that young students need to know the _____ of a rule. Otherwise, they will _____ the rule.

Detail 2 The lecturer made a rule against _____ . The students did not follow the rule _____ . However, after she _____ the purpose of the rule, the students _____ without a problem.

Synthesizing

Give a brief spoken response to the questions based on the reading passage and the lecture.

1   What does the reading passage say about teaching students to follow the rules?

→ *The passage says that it is difficult and that teachers must rely on* _____ .

2   What rule did the instructor create in her elementary school class?

→ *She created a rule against* _____ .

3   What strategy did the instructor use to get her students to follow the rules?

→ *The instructor would* _____ *of the rules to get her students to follow them.*

 **Speaking**

Now give your spoken response for 60 seconds. You may use the guided response to assist you.

?
Question

The professor describes her experience teaching students to follow the rules. Explain how her experience relates to teaching rules.

Guided Response

The reading passage deals with _____ to students. It explains that teachers

must use a variety of _____ to teach students the rules. In the listening,

the lecturer claims that _____ will not follow a rule if they don't know

why it _____. She gives an example to explain. The lecturer made a rule

against _____. At first, the students _____ the

rule. But after she explained the _____ of the rule, the students followed it

_____.

Comparing Listen to a sample response. Then, compare the response with yours.

02-22

FOCUSING ON PRONUNCIATION Practice saying these words using natural intonation.

lesson	respect	variety	exist	purpose
✓	✓	✓	✓	✓

Task 4 History: The American Industrial Revolution

🎯 Vocabulary Take a few moments to review the vocabulary items that will appear in this task.

- **rapid** *adj.* very fast
- **development** *n.* the act of making something larger or more advanced
- **contribute** *v.* to add to something
- **efficient** *adj.* able to work without waste
- **construction** *n.* the act of building something
- **manmade** *adj.* built by human beings; not natural

- **transport** *v.* to move something from one place to another
- **quantity** *n.* a number; an amount
- **raw material** *n.* a basic material used to make something
- **rural** *adj.* of the countryside and not the city

◀ Listening

Listen to a lecture about the American Industrial Revolution. Take notes on key words and concepts in the lecture.

> **Notes**
>
> Topic   *American Industrial Revolution; development of*
>
> Detail 1   *before IR, only traveled on foot or horseback; construction of*
>
>   *made it possible to transport goods to*
>
> Detail 2   *canals could not be built far from water; construction of*
>
>   *moved   of goods than canals; transported goods from*
>
> Key Words   *water and land transportation;*

02-23

Summarizing
Using your own words, summarize the topic of the lecture, describe how the professor explains the topic, and restate the key points.

Topic   The speaker goes over the development of _____ during the American Industrial Revolution.

Detail 1   The country built _____ to transport goods to places far from the _____ . This resulted in _____ on goods and services.

Detail 2   Canals could not be built _____ . So the nation built _____ . Trains could move _____ of goods than canals. They also made it possible to send _____ directly to the North.

Speaking

Now give your spoken response for 60 seconds. You may use the guided response to assist you.

?
Question

Using points and examples from the lecture, explain the developments in transportation during the American Industrial Revolution.

Guided Response

The speaker goes over the development of _____ during the American Industrial

Revolution. Originally, people did not have an _____ way to travel around the

U.S., so the nation constructed _____. These made it possible to _____

_____ goods to places far from the _____ cheaply. Later, the nation

constructed _____. Railroad trains could move _____

than canals. They also made it possible to transport _____ easily from the

South to the North. This lowered _____ further, allowing the U.S. to become

more developed.

Comparing
Listen to a sample response. Then, compare the response with yours.

02-24

⁕FOCUSING ON PARAPHRASING
Read the follow sentences and their paraphrased sentences. Then, practice saying each sentence with natural intonation.

✓ The speaker goes over the development of water and land transportation during the American Industrial Revolution.

→ The topic of the lecture is water and land transportation development during the Industrial Revolution in the U.S.

✓ This resulted in lower prices on goods and services.

→ Due to this, the costs of products and services became cheaper.

✓ They also made it possible to send raw materials directly to the North.

→ Raw materials could be sent directly to the North thanks to railways.

Part B

Chapter 04

Independent Speaking

Task 1 Educational Programs vs. Entertainment Programs

Integrated Speaking

Task 2 Adding Kitchens to Dormitories

Task 3 Psychology: Anchoring Bias

Task 4 Human Biology: Different Types of Tears

Task 1 Educational Programs vs. Entertainment Programs

Warming Up >> Choose a question at random from the list below. Answer the question right away without making notes. Try to speak for at least 10 seconds.

- What are some of your favorite television programs? *I enjoy many different programs such as* Transformers: Prime *and* Stranger Things.
- Which programs are the most popular right now?
- How can watching educational programs improve your life?

Question

Some people prefer to watch educational programs. Others prefer to watch entertainment programs. Which do you think is better and why? Include specific details and reasons in your response.

Brainstorming

Choose one of the two opinions you want to speak about. Then, read over the phrases below. Decide which phrases can be used to support your opinion. Finally, choose the correct words to fill out the idea web.

Choice 1 Educational Programs

▶ **Word List**

- shows on science and history
- programs about engineering
- how to save someone's life
- learn valuable information
- how to escape a burning building
- also cover a variety of topics

▶ **Idea Web**

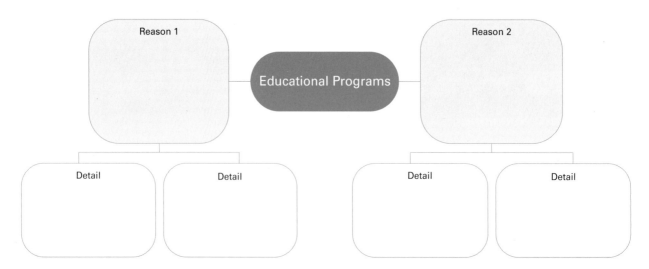

<u>Choice 2</u> **Entertainment Programs**

▶ **Word List**

- not worry about the real world
- clear my head of problems
- want to relax

- can also improve my mood
- watching comedy programs
- helps relieve stress

▶ **Idea Web**

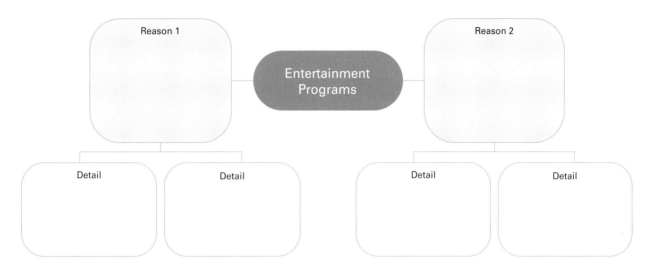

Organizing

Look back at the idea web. Use it to organize your response.

My Choice *Educational Programs / Entertainment Programs*

First Reason

Details

Second Reason

Details

Speaking

Now give your spoken response for 45 seconds. You may use the guided response to assist you.

_____
Guided Response 1 Educational Programs

When I watch television, I mostly watch _____. There are two reasons I feel

this way. First, I can learn _____ from these programs. For instance, one

program taught me how to escape from a _____. I also prefer educational

programs because they cover a _____. Many _____

of educational programs exist. These include programs about science, history, and

_____. On the whole, I feel that it is _____ to watch educational

programs.

_____
Guided Response 2 Entertainment Programs

Although some people enjoy watching educational programs, I prefer watching

_____. To begin with, I want to _____ when I watch television.

I watch TV in order to _____. I don't want to have to worry about the

world and its _____. Furthermore, watching entertainment shows can

_____ my mood. For example, when I watch comedies, I feel happier and

_____. Considering this, I would rather watch entertainment programs than

_____.

_____
Comparing Listen to a sample response. Then, compare the response with yours.

Educational   Entertainment
Programs   Programs

[QR code]   [QR code]
02-25   02-26

Related Topics

Read the following questions related to the topic. For questions 1 to 3, use the information provided to make responses. For questions 4 and 5, use your own ideas to make responses.

1 Children nowadays watch too much television.

Agree	Disagree
- spend hours in front of the television - don't go out and exercise or play with friends	- younger brother and sister rarely watch television - many other entertainment options these days

2 When you watch television programs, do you prefer to see new ones or ones from more than twenty years ago?

New Television Programs	Television Programs from Twenty Years Ago
- know all of the performers - special effects much better	- better storylines then - actors did jobs better in older shows

3 Television programs and movies show too much violence nowadays.

Agree	Disagree
- too much shooting and other violence - people imitate violence in real life	- lots of nonviolent shows on TV - people know programs are not reality

4 Television causes more harm than good.

Agree	Disagree

5 Which do you prefer, watching television programs and movies alone or with your friends?

Alone	With My Friends

Task 2 Adding Kitchens to Dormitories

⊚ Vocabulary   Take a few moments to review the vocabulary items that will appear in this task.

- **force** *v.* to make someone do something that person does not want to do

- **opportunity** *n.* a chance

- **sophomore** *n.* a student in the second year of high school or college

- **suppose** *v.* to believe something to be true

- **breakroom** *n.* an area where people relax

- **unwind** *v.* to relax

- **consider** *v.* to think about carefully

- **unrealistic** *adj.* not realistic; not possible

◀ Reading

Read the following letter to the editor in a university newspaper.

To the Editor,

　The university should add kitchens to the dormitories. Currently, none of the dorms have places to cook. This forces students to eat all of their meals at the cafeterias or at restaurants off campus. If the school installs kitchens, then students will have more eating options available. Students will also have the opportunity to learn how to cook. And they will be able to save money.

Sincerely,

Andrew Ryan, Sophomore

Analyzing   Choose the best answer for each question below.

1   What is the purpose of the letter?

　　Ⓐ To complain about the quality of the cafeteria food

　　Ⓑ To request a change in the university's facilities

　　Ⓒ To give students the opportunity to learn how to cook

2   Why does the letter mention restaurants off campus?

　　Ⓐ To inform students of some good places to eat near the school

　　Ⓑ To show the amount of money students spend on food

　　Ⓒ To explain the food choices that students currently have

3   Which is NOT given as a benefit of cooking in dormitories?

　　Ⓐ Spending less money on food

　　Ⓑ Learning how to cook

　　Ⓒ Eating healthier meals

Listening

Listen to a short conversation related to the reading. Take notes about the woman's opinion.

Notes

The woman (agrees / disagrees) with the letter.

Reason 1 *kitchens have to be installed in breakrooms; students need places to*

Reason 2 *college students are busy; every day go to*

Key Words and Details *students should have kitchens;*

02-27

Summarizing Use the chart below to explain the woman's opinion about the letter.

Main Idea The woman does not believe that the university should _____ in the dorms.

Reason 1 Her first concern is that the kitchens would have to be installed in the _____. This means that students would have no place to _____ after studying.

Reason 2 The woman's second concern is that students _____ to learn how to cook. She claims that students do not have time because they have to _____ and study.

Synthesizing

Give a brief spoken response to the questions based on the letter and the conversation.

1 What is the writer's main argument in the letter?

→ *The writer's main argument is that the university needs to* _____ .

2 How does the man's opinion change during the conversation?

→ *At first, the man supports the plan, but by the end of the conversation, he* _____ .

3 Which claim from the letter does the woman argue against?

→ *The woman argues against the letter's claim that students* _____ *to learn how to cook.*

◀ Speaking

Now give your spoken response for 60 seconds. You may use the guided response to assist you.

? Question

The woman expresses her opinion about the letter to the editor. Explain her opinion and the reasons she gives for holding it.

Guided Response

The man and the woman are talking about a letter asking the university to _____

in the dorms. While the man supports the plan, the woman _____. Her first

argument is that the _____ in the dorms will have to be _____

_____. She feels that students need places to _____ after

studying. Next, the woman claims that college students are _____. She

believes that it is _____ to think that college students have enough time to

_____.

Comparing Listen to a sample response. Then, compare the response with yours.

02-28

⊛ **FOCUSING ON STRESS** Read the following sentences. Be sure to stress the parts in bold.

✓ **If** the **school** in**stalls kitch**ens, then **stu**dents **will have** more eat**ing opt**ions a**vail**able.

✓ **I think** the **wri**ter of **this let**ter **makes** a **good argu**ment.

✓ **We need** a **place** to **un**wind in our **dorms** after **study**ing **all day**.

Task 3 Psychology: Anchoring Bias

🎯 Vocabulary Take a few moments to review the vocabulary items that will appear in this task.

- **topic** *n.* a subject
- **various** *adj.* of many different types or kinds
- **anchor** *n.* a device that keeps someone or something from moving
- **compare** *v.* to look at the similarities and differences between two or more things
- **poor** *adj.* bad; of low quality
- **specialize** *v.* to focus on

- **original** *adj.* relating to the beginning of something
- **impressed** *adj.* feeling deeply or strongly, often in a good way
- **suffer** *v.* to have a sickness, disease, problem, or something similar
- **trust** *v.* to believe

📖 Reading

Read the following passage about anchoring bias.

Anchoring Bias

When people learn about a new topic, they may use various sources of information. However, people often trust the first piece of information they learn about that subject. This acts as an anchor. They then compare all new information they learn about the subject with the first piece of information. This anchoring bias frequently causes people to make poor decisions.

Analyzing Choose the best answer for each question below.

1   What is the main idea of the passage?
- Ⓐ People trust the first thing they learn about a topic.
- Ⓑ Anchoring bias always results in poor decisions.
- Ⓒ Information people learn gets compared to other things.

2   What do people do with the first piece of information they learn?
- Ⓐ Rely completely on it
- Ⓑ Compare it with other information
- Ⓒ Forget about it

3   What is a frequent result of anchoring bias?
- Ⓐ Bad decisions
- Ⓑ Good decisions
- Ⓒ No decisions

◖ Listening

Listen to a short lecture related to the reading. Take notes on key words and specific information from the lecture.

> **Notes**
>
> | Topic | anchoring bias can have results that are _____ |
> |---|---|
> | Detail 1 | purchased a new _____ ; original price was $450; |
> | | was selling for $300; was _____ ; ordered the chair |
> | Detail 2 | wife checked out some websites; found places selling _____ |
> | | suffered from anchoring bias; trusted _____ he learned |
> | Key Words | new office chair; _____ |

02-29

Summarizing Use the chart below to explain the main idea and the key points of the lecture.

Topic The professor talks about a _____ . He says that it shows how _____ does not always have good results.

Detail 1 First, the professor says that he found an office chair online. Its _____ was $450, but it was selling for $300. He ordered the chair and had it _____ .

Detail 2 The professor says that _____ checked some other websites. She found the chair _____ for cheaper prices. The professor had trusted the first piece of information he learned.

◖ Synthesizing

Give a brief spoken response to the questions based on the reading passage and the lecture.

1   According to the reading passage, what is anchoring bias?

→ *Anchoring bias is when a person trusts the first piece of information learned about* _____ .

2   Why did the professor buy the chair?

→ *He saw the original price was* _____ , *but the chair was selling for only* _____ .

3   Why did the professor suffer from anchoring bias?

→ *He* _____ *the first price that he saw and did not check other websites.*

◀ Speaking

Now give your spoken response for 60 seconds. You may use the guided response to assist you.

? Question

The professor describes a personal example. Explain how it is related to anchoring bias.

Guided Response

The professor talks about buying an _____. He says he found a chair online. It

was selling for a _____, so he bought it. Later, the _____

searched some other _____. She found the chair available for even

_____. In this case, the professor trusted the first information he learned

about the chair. That was an example of _____. In anchoring bias, a person

_____ the first information learned to other information. In this case, the

professor had a _____.

Comparing Listen to a sample response. Then, compare the response with yours.

02-30

☆FOCUSING ON PRONUNCIATION Practice saying these words using natural intonation.

office	available	trust	anchoring	compare
✓	✓	✓	✓	✓

Task 4 Human Biology: Different Types of Tears

🎯 Vocabulary Take a few moments to review the vocabulary items that will appear in this task.

- **lifetime** *n.* the time during which a person is alive
- **blink** *v.* to close and then open one's eyes quickly
- **dust** *n.* very small dry powder
- **substance** *n.* a material of a certain type
- **bacterial infection** *n.* a disease caused by germs that enter the body

- **immune system** *n.* the system that protects one's body from diseases
- **joy** *n.* extreme happiness
- **protein** *n.* a substance in milk, meat, and other foods that is important for the human diet
- **painkiller** *n.* something that reduces pain

◀ Listening

Listen to a lecture on the topic of different types of tears. Take notes on key words and concepts in the lecture.

Notes	
Topic	*different types of*
Detail 1	*blinking tears; keep eye moist and*
	fight against
Detail 2	*crying tears; produced when we feel*
	contain proteins and natural
Key Words	*several types of tears;*

02-31

Summarizing Using your own words, summarize the topic of the lecture, describe how the professor explains the topic, and restate the key points.

Topic In the listening passage, the professor talks about   of tears.

Detail 1 The first type of tears is   . These keep the eyes   and remove dust. They also fight against   .

Detail 2 The other type of tears is   . These are produced when we feel   . These contain proteins and act as   .

Speaking

Now give your spoken response for 60 seconds. You may use the guided response to assist you.

? Question

Using points and examples from the talk, explain the different types of tears.

Guided Response

The professor's lecture focuses on two different types of _____. The first type of

tears she discusses is _____. These tears are _____

when we blink. They keep the _____ and remove dust. Blinking tears are also

part of our _____ as they help fight against _____.

The professor then talks about _____. These are produced whenever we feel

_____. Crying tears contain proteins and _____.

Producing crying tears helps us _____.

Comparing Listen to a sample response. Then, compare the response with yours.

02-32

⚬ FOCUSING ON PARAPHRASING
Read the follow sentences and their paraphrased sentences. Then, practice saying each sentence with natural intonation.

✓ The professor's lecture focuses on two different types of tears.

→ The lecturer mainly discusses two sorts of tears, blinking tears and crying tears.

✓ linking tears are also part of our immune system as they help fight against bacterial infections.

→ Blinking tears work with our immune system to prevent diseases in the eyes.

✓ These are produced whenever we feel strong emotions.

→ Whenever we feel very happy or sad, our eyes make crying tears.

Part B

Chapter 05

Independent Speaking

Task 1 Spending Vacations at Home vs. Traveling

Integrated Speaking

Task 2 School Newspaper No Longer to Be Printed

Task 3 Animal Science: Echolocation

Task 4 Business: Ineffective Logos

Task 1 Spending Vacations at Home vs. Traveling

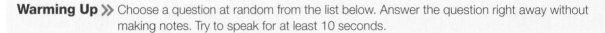

Warming Up >> Choose a question at random from the list below. Answer the question right away without making notes. Try to speak for at least 10 seconds.

- How did you spend your last vacation? *I went on a trip with my family. We visited the Philippines.*

- Do you prefer relaxing during your vacations or doing many activities?

- How can traveling during vacation be stressful?

? Question

Some people prefer to spend their vacations at home. Others prefer to travel. Explain which you prefer and why. Use specific reasons and examples to support your preference.

Brainstorming

Choose one of the two opinions you want to speak about. Then, read over the phrases below. Decide which phrases can be used to support your opinion. Finally, choose the correct words to fill out the idea web.

Choice 1 Staying at Home

▶ **Word List**

- do not have to pay for attractions
- can also save money
- is more relaxing
- spend all day lying in bed
- plane tickets and hotels are expensive
- read books and play video games

▶ **Idea Web**

Choice 2 **Traveling**

▶ **Word List**

- experience new places
- can escape from my regular life
- meet many new people
- is also a lot of fun
- swim in the ocean
- visit amusement parks

▶ **Idea Web**

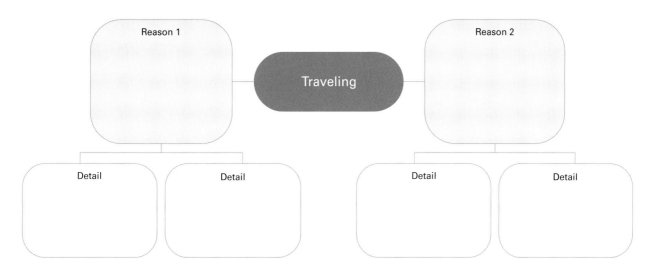

◖ **Organizing**

Look back at the idea web. Use it to organize your response.

My Choice *Staying at Home / Traveling*

First Reason

Details

Second Reason

Details

Speaking

Now give your spoken response for 45 seconds. You may use the guided response to assist you.

Guided Response 1 Staying at Home

During my time off from school, I enjoy staying _____. I feel this way for

two reasons. The first is that staying at home is _____. I can read books,

play _____, or do nothing at all. I also prefer staying home because it

_____. Vacations can _____ thousands of dollars.

To me, this is a _____ of money. On the whole, I would much rather

_____ during vacation.

Guided Response 2 Traveling

I like to _____ whenever I have time off. For one, traveling gives me

the chance to _____ from my regular life. I can experience new and

_____. Another reason I like traveling is that it is _____.

I can visit an amusement park or swim in _____. This is more _____

_____ than staying at home. Some people may enjoy staying home when they have

time off. As for me, _____ is much better.

Comparing Listen to a sample response. Then, compare the response with yours.

Staying at Home

02-33

Traveling

02-34

◀ Related Topics

Read the following questions related to the topic. For questions 1 to 3, use the information provided to make responses. For questions 4 and 5, use your own ideas to make responses.

1 Which do you prefer, to take trips in your own country or to travel to a foreign country?

Take Trips in My Own Country	Travel to a Foreign Country
- many nice places to see - can save money	- visit exotic places - see places that were important in history

2 Everyone should take at least one trip abroad.

Agree	Disagree
- can experience other cultures - experience spending time in other lands	- no need to travel far from home - too expensive to travel abroad for most people

3 When you have vacation, do you prefer to spend time outdoors or to remain indoors?

Spend Time Outdoors	Remain Indoors
- exercise and get in good shape - meet friends by going out	- prefer to read books at home - don't have an active lifestyle

4 Vacation is a time when people should try to improve themselves.

Agree	Disagree

5 It is better to take long trips than to take short ones.

Agree	Disagree

Task 2 School Newspaper No Longer to Be Printed

◎ Vocabulary   Take a few moments to review the vocabulary items that will appear in this task.

- **print** *v.* to produce by putting written words onto paper

- **ink** *n.* a liquid used for writing and printing

- **drastically** *adv.* greatly; very much

- **version** *n.* a certain form or type of something

- **cease** *v.* to stop; to halt

- **edition** *n.* the format in which something is published

- **budget** *n.* an amount of money that can be spent in a certain period of time

- **entirely** *adv.* completely; fully

- **especially** *adv.* particularly

- **physical** *adj.* relating to something material

■ Reading

Read the following announcement from a university.

School Newspaper to Stop Being Printed

Beginning this Monday, the school newspaper will no longer be printed. Instead, students can read the newspaper online. Lately, the prices of ink and paper have increased drastically. In addition, few people actually read the printed version anymore. So the school has decided no longer to print it. If you have any questions regarding this matter, please call 494-3933 and ask to speak to Margaret Taylor.

Analyzing   Choose the best answer for each question below.

1   What is the purpose of the announcement?
  Ⓐ To ask students to sign up to write for a newspaper
  Ⓑ To inform students about a change to a newspaper
  Ⓒ To announce that students must pay for a newspaper

2   Why is the school making the change?
  Ⓐ Because some material is too expensive
  Ⓑ Because students requested the change
  Ⓒ Because technology has improved lately

3   Which of the following is true according to the announcement?
  Ⓐ The newspaper will shut down when the semester ends.
  Ⓑ Not many people read the printed paper nowadays.
  Ⓒ Students can send an email if they have questions.

Listening

Listen to a short conversation related to the reading. Take notes about the man's opinion.

> **Notes**
>
> The man (likes / dislikes / has mixed feelings about) the university's plan.
>
> Reason *school has budget problems; papers are expensive to print; good idea to*
>
> *go online;*
>
> Key Words and Details *have mixed feelings;*

02-35

Summarizing Use the chart below to explain the man's opinion about the announcement.

Main Idea The man has mixed feelings. He understands why the university made the decision, but he is not completely _____.

Reason 1 The school has _____, and printing a newspaper is expensive. So it's a good idea to _____ if _____ are reading the paper.

Reason 2 He likes _____ a physical newspaper and reading it. Doing that is a better _____ for him than reading online.

Synthesizing

Give a brief spoken response to the questions based on the announcement and the conversation.

1 According to the announcement, what will happen this Monday?

→ *The school will stop* _____ *the school newspaper.*

2 How does the man feeling about the announcement?

→ *The man says that he has* _____ *about the announcement.*

3 What does the man say he often does during lunch?

→ *He says that he often reads a* _____ *during lunch.*

Speaking

Now give your spoken response for 60 seconds. You may use the guided response to assist you.

? Question

The man expresses his opinion about the announcement by the school. Explain his opinion and the reasons he gives for holding it.

Guided Response

The speakers talk about the school's decision to _____ the school newspaper. The man has mixed feelings about this decision. First, he understands the decision because printing a paper is _____. He mentions that the school has _____. So he thinks it is smart to stop printing the paper since _____ are reading it. However, he comments that he also dislikes the decision. For him, reading a _____ is better than reading the _____ of the paper.

Comparing Listen to a sample response. Then, compare the response with yours.

02-36

⊕ **FOCUSING ON STRESS** Read the following sentences. Be sure to stress the parts in bold.

✓ The **man** has **mix**ed **feel**ings about **this** de**ci**sion.

✓ He under**stands** the de**ci**sion be**cau**se **print**ing a **pa**per is ex**pen**sive.

✓ He **com**ments that he **al**so dis**likes** the de**ci**sion.

Task 3 Animal Science: Echolocation

🎯 Vocabulary Take a few moments to review the vocabulary items that will appear in this task.

- **process** *n.* a series of actions that lead to a wanted result
- **constantly** *adv.* at all times; continually
- **reflect** *v.* to bounce back
- **environment** *n.* the area surrounding something

- **hunt** *v.* to chase and kill an animal for food
- **high-pitched** *adj.* making a high sound
- **image** *n.* the thought of how something looks or might look
- **sensitive** *adj.* able to sense very small changes in something

Reading

Read the following passage about echolocation.

Echolocation

Most animals rely on their sight to understand their environment. However, some animals are different. They rely on their hearing instead of their sight. They do this through a process called echolocation. These animals constantly give off sounds as they travel through an area. The sounds reflect off the objects in the environment. The animals hear these sounds and understand the shape of the surrounding area. By using echolocation, these animals are also able to hunt for food.

Analyzing Choose the best answer for each question below.

1 What is the main idea of the passage?
   Ⓐ Most flying animals rely on echolocation to travel around.
   Ⓑ Sounds can help animals move through an area more quickly.
   Ⓒ Certain animals use sound rather than sight to understand the world.

2 What is the first step in the echolocation process?
   Ⓐ An animal gives off sounds.
   Ⓑ An animal learns the shape of the area.
   Ⓒ Sounds reflect off objects.

3 Which of the following is true according to the passage?
   Ⓐ Animals can use echolocation to find food.
   Ⓑ Animals that use echolocation are not able to see very well.
   Ⓒ Animals that use echolocation constantly make sounds.

Listening

Listen to a short lecture related to the reading. Take notes on key words and specific information from the lecture.

Notes

Topic	*bats use*
Detail 1	*live in dark places; make*
	sounds shoot out like
Detail 2	*figure out where sounds come from and how long they take to come back; create*
	sensitive enough to find
Key Words	*high-pitched sounds;*

02-37

Summarizing Use the chart below to explain the main idea and the key points of the lecture.

Topic The instructor mainly talks about how bats _____ .

Detail 1 She begins by describing the _____ sounds bats make. She explains that they shoot out like _____ and bounce back to the bats.

Detail 2 The bats figure out _____ the sounds are coming from and _____ it takes for them to come back. This way, the bats can create an _____ of their environment. They can also _____ in this way.

Synthesizing

Give a brief spoken response to the questions based on the reading passage and the lecture.

1 How do animals use echolocation according to the reading passage?

→ *They use echolocation to understand the shape of an area and to* _____ .

2 What happens to the sounds created by bats when they fly?

→ *The sounds created by bats shoot out like lasers and* _____ .

3 What type of animals can bats hunt using echolocation?

→ *Bats use echolocation to hunt* _____ .

 **Speaking**

Now give your spoken response for 60 seconds. You may use the guided response to assist you.

? Question

The professor describes the concept of echolocation by giving one example. Explain the example and how it illustrates the concept of echolocation.

Guided Response

The reading passage and the lecture both deal with the topic of _____ . The

passage gives some background _____ about the topic. The instructor

explains this topic by talking about _____ . According to the instructor, bats

make _____ sounds when they fly. These sounds shoot out like lasers and

_____ to the bats. The bats can use these sounds to create an image of their

_____ . She also mentions that bats hunt _____ by

using echolocation.

Comparing Listen to a sample response. Then, compare the response with yours.

02-38

environment	reflect	high-pitched	image	sensitive
✓	✓	✓	✓	✓

Task 4 Business: Ineffective Logos

🎯 Vocabulary   Take a few moments to review the vocabulary items that will appear in this task.

- **grab** *v.* to get the attention of somebody
- **emotion** *n.* a strong feeling
- **apparently** *adv.* seemingly; clearly
- **go out of business** *exp.* to stop doing business

- **appearance** *n.* the way someone or something looks
- **match** *v.* to go well with something
- **old fashioned** *adj.* of or relating to the past; outdated
- **immediately** *adv.* without delay; right away

◀ Listening

Listen to a lecture on the topic of ineffective logos. Take notes on key words and concepts in the lecture.

Notes

Topic	*effective logos grab our attention and make us want to buy the product; but*
Detail 1	*different colors create different emotions; choosing _____ is important*
	healthcare company had a _____ logo; went out of
Detail 2	*appearance of logo also important; should match*
	computer company had _____ logo; customers thought their products were
Key Words	*grabs attention; not all logos effective;*

02-39

Summarizing   Using your own words, summarize the topic of the lecture, describe how the professor explains the topic, and restate the key points.

Topic   The professor discusses _____ product logos in his lecture.

Detail 1   The _____ of a logo is a very important. One healthcare company had a _____ . Black is the color of _____ . So the company went _____ .

Detail 2   The _____ of a logo also matters. The logo should _____ the company's products. A small computer company had an _____ logo. So people thought its _____ were outdated. It made a more _____ , and the business became successful.

◖ Speaking

Now give your spoken response for 60 seconds. You may use the guided response to assist you.

?
Question

Using points and examples from the lecture, explain how logos can be ineffective.

Guided Response

The professor talks about _____ product logos in his lecture. He first mentions

the importance of _____. He describes a _____

that had a black logo. Black is the color of _____. As a result, the company

_____. Next, the professor talks about logo _____.

He describes a computer company with an _____ logo. People saw the

logo and thought the company's products were _____. So it made a

_____ logo. Afterward, it became _____.

Comparing Listen to a sample response. Then, compare the response with yours.

02-40

FOCUSING ON PARAPHRASING Read the follow sentences and their paraphrased sentences. Then, practice saying each sentence with natural intonation.

✓ The professor talks about ineffective product logos in his lecture.

→ In the lecture, the speaker describes logos that did not work.

✓ As a result, the company went out of business.

→ Consequently, the company had to close its business.

✓ People saw the logo and thought the company's products were outdated.

→ Customers believed the company's products were out of date based on the logo.

Part B

Chapter 06

Independent Speaking

Task 1   Store-Bought Presents vs. Homemade Presents

Integrated Speaking

Task 2   Moving Student Orientation

Task 3   Sociology: Sibling Rivalry

Task 4   Animal Science: Earthworms Help Plant Growth

Task 1 Store-Bought Presents vs. Homemade Presents

Warming Up >> Choose a question at random from the list below. Answer the question right away without making notes. Try to speak for at least 10 seconds.

- What is the best present you have ever received? *The best present I have ever received was a new laptop from my parents.*
- Do you think that a good present is an expensive present?
- What are some homemade presents that you have received in the past?

Question

Would you rather receive store-bought presents or homemade presents? Include specific details and reasons in your response.

Brainstorming

Choose one of the two opinions you want to speak about. Then, read over the phrases below. Decide which phrases can be used to support your opinion. Finally, choose the correct words to fill out the idea web.

Choice 1 Store-Bought Presents

▶ **Word List**

- also more practical
- come in a wider variety
- use new television for years

- homemade gifts used a few times
- designer clothing
- cellphones and other electronics

▶ **Idea Web**

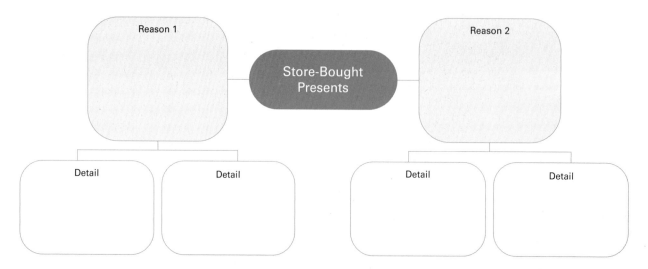

<u>Choice 2</u> **Homemade Presents**

▶ **Word List**

- have special meanings
- care about me very much
- cannot buy in store

- also made especially for me
- sister made chocolates
- takes time to make gift

▶ **Idea Web**

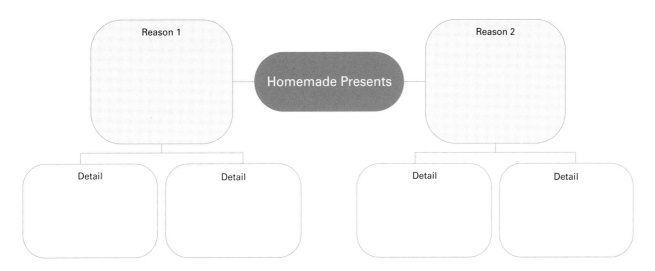

■ **Organizing**

Look back at the idea web. Use it to organize your response.

My Choice *Store-Bought Presents / Homemade Presents*

First Reason

Details

Second Reason

Details

Speaking

Now give your spoken response for 45 seconds. You may use the guided response to assist you.

Guided Response 1 Store-Bought Presents

I enjoy receiving homemade presents. Nevertheless, I prefer _____. I feel this

way for two reasons. For starters, store-bought gifts come in a _____ than

homemade gifts. To be specific, I can receive anything from a _____ to a

brand-new car. My second reason is that store-bought gifts tend to be more _____

_____. For example, I can receive a high-definition television that I can use

_____ for years. However, most homemade gifts can only be used

_____.

Guided Response 2 Homemade Presents

Most people prefer store-bought presents. However, I would rather receive _____.

First of all, homemade presents have _____. I know the person spent a lot

of time making the gift, so that means that the person _____ about me very

much. Another reason I prefer homemade presents is that they are made _____

for me. To give an example, my sister made _____ for me. I cannot

_____ these in a store, so her gift was very special to me.

Comparing Listen to a sample response. Then, compare the response with yours.

Store-Bought
Presents

Homemade
Presents

02-41

02-42

Related Topics

Read the following questions related to the topic. For questions 1 to 3, use the information provided to make responses. For questions 4 and 5, use your own ideas to make responses.

1 It is important to have a birthday party every year.

Agree	Disagree
- spend time with friends and family members - receive presents	- don't enjoy celebrating my birthday - would rather just have dinner with my family

2 A person should always buy a gift for a friend on that person's birthday.

Agree	Disagree
- good manners - can show your friend how much you care	- friends don't need to buy presents for each other - may not have time to buy a present

3 When you attend a birthday party, do you prefer to go to a person's home or to go out somewhere?

Go to a Person's Home	Go Out Somewhere
- fewer people = better atmosphere - more comfortable at a person's home	- can enjoy a meal at a restaurant - can choose a central location easy for everyone to get to

4 Children should invite everyone in their class to their birthday party.

Agree	Disagree

5 Would you rather receive one big present or many smaller ones for your birthday?

One Big Present	Many Smaller Presents

Task 2 Moving Student Orientation

⊚ Vocabulary Take a few moments to review the vocabulary items that will appear in this task.

- **orientation** *n.* the time when new students are introduced to their school

- **transition** *v.* to change from one condition to another

- **enjoyable** *adj.* pleasurable; agreeable

- **forthcoming** *adj.* upcoming

- **freshman** *n.* a student in the first year of high school or university

- **fine** *adj.* good; acceptable

- **deserted** *adj.* without people; abandoned

- **ghost town** *n.* a town that no longer has any people living in it

◀ Reading

Read the following letter to the editor from a university student.

To the Editor,

   I am writing this letter to make a request to the university. I believe the school should move the orientation for new students from the fall to the summer. Having the orientation during the summer will give new students more time to transition into university life. On top of this, the weather is nicer, making it more enjoyable to visit the campus. I hope the university will change the orientation to summer this forthcoming school year.

Juliana Goldman
Freshman

Analyzing Choose the best answer for each question below.

1   What is the purpose of the letter?

   Ⓐ To complain about the school's orientation program

   Ⓑ To create a second orientation program during the summer

   Ⓒ To ask the university to change the time of the orientation program

2   Which of the following is true according to the letter?

   Ⓐ Orientation currently takes place during the fall.

   Ⓑ Some new students requested having orientation during the summer.

   Ⓒ The school has decided to create a summer orientation.

3   What is one of the arguments given in favor of a summer orientation?

   Ⓐ Incoming students will have more time to get used to college life.

   Ⓑ Other universities have their orientation programs during the summer.

   Ⓒ The weather is too hot for orientation during the summer.

Listening

Listen to a short conversation related to the reading. Take notes about the man's opinion.

> **Notes**
>
> The man (agrees / disagrees) with the letter.
>
> Reason 1 *campus is practically deserted; most students are* ....
>
> ....
>
> Reason 2 *most people go on vacation during summer; students cannot* ....
>
> ....
>
> Key Words and Details *having the orientation during fall is fine; campus deserted;* ....
>
> ....

02-43

Summarizing Use the chart below to explain the man's opinion about the letter.

Main Idea   The man feels that having the orientation during the fall is ....
In this way, he .... with the letter.

Reason 1   For his first argument, the man states that the campus is ....
during the summer. Because of this, the students cannot see what the campus is
....

Reason 2   The man also notes that most people .... during the
summer. This means they cannot .... to orientation during
the summer, making the orientation ....

Synthesizing

Give a brief spoken response to the questions based on the letter and the conversation.

1   According to the letter, how would having orientation during the summer benefit new students?

→ *It would benefit new students by giving them more time to* .... *into college life.*

2   What does the woman say about the university during the summer?

→ *The woman says that the campus is practically a* ....

3   How does the man feel about the number of students who can attend summer orientation?

→ *He feels that most students* .... *because they will be on vacation.*

Speaking

Now give your spoken response for 60 seconds. You may use the guided response to assist you.

? Question

The man expresses his opinion about the student's letter. Explain his opinion and his reasons for thinking that way.

Guided Response

The man feels that the orientation should remain in the _____ . His first argument is that the campus is mostly _____ during the summer. The man claims that most students are _____ and that many _____ are closed. As a result, the students will not see what the campus is _____ . The man then points out that most people go _____ during the summer. This means that most students will not be able to _____ in a summer orientation program.

Comparing Listen to a sample response. Then, compare the response with yours.

02-44

⊛**FOCUSING ON STRESS** Read the following sentences. Be sure to stress the parts in bold.

✓ I **hope** the university will **change** the or**ien**ta**tion** to sum**mer** this **forth**coming **school year**.

✓ The **school** ba**si**cally be**comes** a **ghost town**.

✓ **Most peo**ple go on va**ca**tion **dur**ing the sum**mer**, **don't they**?

Task 3 Sociology: Sibling Rivalry

🎯 **Vocabulary** Take a few moments to review the vocabulary items that will appear in this task.

- **competition** *n.* the act of trying to win something
- **jealousy** *n.* an unhappy feeling of wanting to have something that somebody else has
- **severe** *adj.* very bad, serious, or unpleasant
- **peace** *n.* a time without fighting

- **recognize** *v.* to give special attention
- **unique** *adj.* belonging to only one person; one of a kind
- **athlete** *n.* a person who is good at sports
- **compromise** *n.* an agreement in which each group gives up something wanted

▌ Reading

Read the following passage about sibling rivalry.

Sibling Rivalry

Sibling rivalry is a type of competition between brothers and sisters. Children fight for the attention of their parents. They often develop a sense of jealousy toward each other. Sibling rivalries usually begin around the age of five. Rivalries often continue into the teenage years. In severe cases, sibling rivalries continue into adulthood. Fortunately for parents, there are several methods that can reduce sibling rivalries.

Analyzing Choose the best answer for each question below.

1 What is the purpose of the passage?
  Ⓐ To introduce a concept in child psychology
  Ⓑ To teach parents how to deal with sibling rivalries
  Ⓒ To explain changes that happen as children grow up

2 What do children usually fight over in a sibling rivalry?
  Ⓐ The attention of their parents
  Ⓑ Feelings of jealousy
  Ⓒ Each other's attention

3 Which of the following is true according to the passage?
  Ⓐ Parents cannot do anything to reduce sibling rivalries.
  Ⓑ Sibling rivalries usually last until adulthood.
  Ⓒ Children feel envious toward their siblings.

◀ Listening

Listen to a short lecture related to the reading. Take notes on key words and specific information from the lecture.

Notes

Topic   *dealing with*

Detail 1   *recognize each son's unique abilities; one son was an*

Detail 2   *let children work out differences themselves; even young children*

Key Words   *boys fought all the time; caused family a lot of stress;*

02-45

Summarizing Use the chart below to explain the main idea and the key points of the lecture.

Topic   The professor talks about methods to _____ sibling rivalry.

Detail 1 The first method the professor used was _____ each son's
          abilities. She praised both boys for their _____. This made them
          both _____.

Detail 2 The professor also let her children _____ their differences
          themselves. She explains that even young children are able to make
          _____.

◀ Synthesizing

Give a brief spoken response to the questions based on the reading passage and the lecture.

1   How do children in a sibling rivalry usually feel toward each other?

    → *They often develop feelings of* _____ *toward each other.*

2   How did sibling rivalry affect the professor's family?

    → *The sibling rivalry between the professor's sons caused her family* _____.

3   What did the professor's sons feel when they received praise for their unique abilities?

    → *Praising the sons for their talents made them both* _____.

Speaking

Now give your spoken response for 60 seconds. You may use the guided response to assist you.

? Question

The professor describes two methods that can reduce sibling rivalry. Explain the methods and how they reduce sibling rivalry.

Guided Response

The reading passage describes _____. This is a type of _____ between brothers and sisters. They often fight for the _____ of their parents. In her lecture, the professor describes _____ she used to reduce sibling rivalry between her sons. The first method was recognizing the _____ of her sons. She gave both boys praise. This made them both _____. Her second method was to let her sons work out their _____ themselves. The professor explains that even young children are able to make _____.

Comparing Listen to a sample response. Then, compare the response with yours.

02-46

⭐ **FOCUSING ON PRONUNCIATION** Practice saying these words by using natural intonation.

rivalry	jealousy	severe	athlete	compromise
✓	✓	✓	✓	✓

Task 4 Animal Science: Earthworms Help Plant Growth

🎯 **Vocabulary** Take a few moments to review the vocabulary items that will appear in this task.

- **pest** *n.* an animal that damages plants
- **nutrient** *n.* a substance that plants, animals, and people need to live and grow
- **organic** *adj.* of living things
- **dropping** *n.* solid waste from an animal
- **crawl** *v.* to move with the body close to the ground

- **fertilizer** *n.* a substance added to soil to help plants grow
- **topsoil** *n.* the upper layer of dirt
- **vice versa** *adv.* in reverse order from what is stated; conversely
- **introduce** *v.* to bring something to a place for the first time

◀ **Listening** ▶

Listen to a lecture on the topic of earthworms. Take notes on key words and concepts in the lecture.

> **Notes**
>
> Topic   *earthworms; help plants _____ ; help keep soil _____*
>
> Detail 1   *increase the amount of nutrients in the soil*
>
>   *break down _____ into nutrients plants can use; worm droppings*
>
> Detail 2   *create topsoil*
>
>   *move _____ of dirt to top; increases air in soil and*
>
>   *tunnels allow water to _____*
>
> Key Words   *increase nutrients in soil; organic materials;*

02-47

Summarizing Using your own words, summarize the topic of the lecture, describe how the professor explains the topic, and restate the key points.

Topic   In the lecture, the instructor explains how earthworms help _____ grow. He says they do this by keeping the soil _____ .

Detail 1   The first way they do this is by increasing the amount of _____ in the soil. They eat leaves and grass and break them down into _____ plants can use. This happens because worms leave their _____ in the soil.

Detail 2   Worms also create _____ . As they crawl through the dirt, worms move the _____ of soil to the top. This introduces more _____ into the soil. Their tunnels also allow more _____ to pass through the soil easily.

◀ Speaking

Now give your spoken response for 60 seconds. You may use the guided response to assist you.

? Question

Using points and examples from the lecture, explain how earthworms help plants grow.

Guided Response

The instructor explains how earthworms help _____ by keeping the soil healthy.

For one, earthworms increase the amount of _____ in the soil. They eat

_____ such as leaves and grass. Later, their droppings act as an _____

_____ . The instructor then talks about how worms create _____ .

He says that worms move the _____ of soil to the top as they crawl through

the soil. This introduces more _____ and nutrients into the soil. Their

_____ also help water pass through the soil.

Comparing Listen to a sample response. Then, compare the response with yours.

02-48

⊛ FOCUSING ON PARAPHRASING Read the follow sentences and their paraphrased sentences. Then, practice saying each sentence with natural intonation.

✓ The instructor explains how earthworms help plants grow by keeping the soil healthy.

→ The professor talks about how earthworms improve soil and keep plants healthy.

✓ They eat organic materials such as leaves and grass.

→ The worms eat leaves, grass, and other natural materials.

✓ He says that worms move the lower layers of soil to the top as they crawl through the soil.

→ As worms move through the dirt, they bring lower layers to the top.

Part B

Chapter 07

Independent Speaking

Task 1 Students Should Have Part-Time Job Experience

Integrated Speaking

Task 2 Fitness Center Renovation

Task 3 Business: Giving Samples

Task 4 Agriculture: Organic Farming

Task 1 Students Should Have Part-Time Job Experience

Warming Up >> Choose a question at random from the list below. Answer the question right away without making notes. Try to speak for at least 10 seconds.

- What can students learn from having a job? *Students can learn about using their time well. They can also learn about making and spending money.*
- How can having a job make it more difficult to study?
- How much money can a student probably save by working at a part-time job?

? Question

Do you agree or disagree with the following statement? Students should have part-time job experience before entering university. Include specific details and reasons in your response.

Brainstorming

Choose one of the two opinions you want to speak about. Then, read over the phrases below. Decide which phrases can be used to support your opinion. Finally, choose the correct words to fill out the idea web.

Choice 1 Have Part-Time Job Experience

▶ **Word List**

- teaches time-management skills
- students usually do not have much money
- live without wasting money
- also learn value of money
- balance working and studying
- learn to study efficiently

▶ **Idea Web**

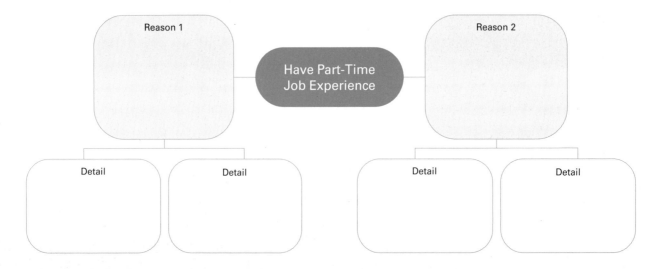

Choice 2 **Focus on Studying**

▶ **Word List**

- little economic benefit
- cannot get scholarships with poor grades
- also do not pay high salaries
- working students have lower grades
- cannot save much money
- should focus on getting good grades

▶ **Idea Web**

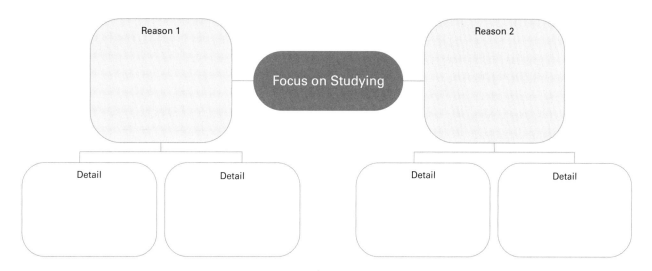

⬛ Organizing

Look back at the idea web. Use it to organize your response.

My Choice *Have Part-Time Job Experience / Focus on Studying*

First Reason

Details

Second Reason

Details

◀ Speaking

Now give your spoken response for 45 seconds. You may use the guided response to assist you.

Guided Response 1 Have Part-Time Job Experience

I am convinced that students should have _____ before going to college.

First of all, I believe that having a job teaches students _____ . Students with

jobs learn how to _____ their work time and study time. I also believe that

work experience helps students because it teaches them the _____ . Working

students learn how to live without _____ money. This is important because

most college students do not have _____ money.

Guided Response 2 Focus on Studying

I disagree that students should have _____ before entering college. Instead,

I believe that students should focus _____ . First, the main responsibility of

students is getting _____ . However, students who have part-time jobs usually

have _____ than students who do not work. On top of this, most part-time jobs

do not pay _____ . So there is little _____ for students

to work at these jobs. Overall, I strongly believe that students should _____ only

on studying.

Comparing Listen to a sample response. Then, compare the response with yours.

Have Part-Time
Job Experience

02-49

Focus on
Studying

02-50

Related Topics

Read the following questions related to the topic. For questions 1 to 3, use the information provided to make responses. For questions 4 and 5, use your own ideas to make responses.

1 University students should have part-time jobs related to their majors.

Agree	Disagree
- makes jobs more interesting - can help students get full-time jobs after graduating	- should take jobs that pay the most - don't really learn much from part-time jobs

2 High school students should only work part time on weekends.

Agree	Disagree
- need to study on weekdays - more productive use of time on weekends	- is okay to work a couple of hours on weekday evenings - some jobs require students to work from Monday to Friday

3 Which would you prefer, a part-time job working indoors or outdoors?

Working Indoors	Working Outdoors
- want an office job - prefer to sit down while working	- enjoy spending time outdoors - can get in shape while working

4 High school students should only be allowed to work ten or few hours a week at their part-time jobs.

Agree	Disagree

5 Part-time workers do not get paid enough by their employers.

Agree	Disagree

Task 2 Fitness Center Renovation

🎯 **Vocabulary** Take a few moments to review the vocabulary items that will appear in this task.

- **renovate** *v.* to make changes and repairs to an old building so that it is in good condition
- **enlarge** *v.* to make something bigger
- **apologize** *v.* to say that one is sorry for doing something wrong

- **inconvenience** *n.* trouble; problems
- **work out** *phr v.* to exercise
- **take** *v.* to think about; to consider

◼ Reading

Read the following announcement from a university.

Fitness Center Renovation

This is a notice to all City University students. From February 1 to July 31, the Blatt Fitness Center will be closed. The fitness center no longer meets the needs of our students. Therefore, the school has decided to renovate the facility. The exercise areas and the locker rooms will be enlarged. During this time, a swimming pool will also be constructed. We apologize for any inconveniences this may cause.

Analyzing Choose the best answer for each question below.

1   What is the purpose of the announcement?
   Ⓐ To inform students about a change in the school schedule
   Ⓑ To let students know about the closure of a campus facility
   Ⓒ To announce the opening of a new fitness center on campus

2   Why is the university renovating the fitness center?
   Ⓐ Because it is inconvenient
   Ⓑ Because it was built a long time ago
   Ⓒ Because it is too small

3   What will be added to the fitness center?
   Ⓐ Exercise areas
   Ⓑ A swimming pool
   Ⓒ Locker rooms

Listening

Listen to a short conversation related to the reading. Take notes about the woman's opinion.

Notes

The woman (agrees / disagrees) with the announcement.

Reason 1 *exercise machines are really old; usually*

Reason 2 *facilities are too small; university has*

Key Words and Details *renovating for the best;*

02-51

Summarizing Use the chart below to explain the woman's opinion about the announcement.

Main Idea The woman believes the renovations are _____.

Reason 1 First, the woman explains that most of the exercise machines are _____. A lot of times, they are _____. This makes it hard to get a _____.

Reason 2 Next, the woman argues that the facilities are _____. She notes that the university has many _____ than it used to. As a result, the fitness center is always _____.

Synthesizing

Give a brief spoken response to the questions based on the announcement and the conversation.

1 How will the renovations change the fitness center?

→ *The renovations will make the exercise areas and the* _____ *larger.*

2 According to the woman, why does the fitness center no longer meet the needs of students?

→ *She states that the university has* _____ *than it used to.*

3 How does the man support the woman's argument?

→ *He says that he usually has to wait to use* _____ .

◀ Speaking

Now give your spoken response for 60 seconds. You may use the guided response to assist you.

? Question

The woman expresses her opinion of the announcement. Explain her opinion and the reasons she gives for holding it.

Guided Response

The speakers are discussing their university's plan to _____ the fitness center. The woman feels the plan is _____ . She gives two reasons to _____ her opinion. The first is that the _____ are very old. She claims that the machines are usually _____ . This makes it hard to get a _____ . Furthermore, the woman says that the facilities are _____ . The university has _____ than it used to, so the fitness center is always _____ .

Comparing Listen to a sample response. Then, compare the response with yours.

02-52

⊙ **FOCUSING ON STRESS** Read the following sentences. Be sure to stress the parts in bold.

✓ The **fit**ness cen**ter** is **go**ing to be **closed** the en**tire** se**mes**ter.

✓ **I think** re**no**va**t**ing the **fit**ness **cen**ter is for **the best**.

✓ The **uni**ver**sity** has ma**ny more** stu**dents now** than it **used to**.

Task 3 Business: Giving Samples

🎯 **Vocabulary** Take a few moments to review the vocabulary items that will appear in this task.

- **continually** *adv.* happening all the time
- **skeptical** *adj.* having doubt about a statement
- **overcome** *v.* to defeat someone or something
- **expose** *v.* to cause to be visible; to show
- **risk** *n.* the possibility that something bad will happen

- **struggle** *v.* to try very hard to deal with something difficult
- **profit** *n.* money made by a business
- **browse** *v.* to look at many things in a store to find something worth buying
- **realize** *v.* to come to believe; to recognize

Reading

Read the following passage about giving samples.

Giving Samples

The success of a product or business depends on continually selling more products. This is often quite difficult because customers are skeptical of trying new products. They do not want to buy a product they are not familiar with. However, businesses can overcome this by offering free samples. Offering free samples exposes a product to new people. It also gives customers a chance to try a product without taking the risk of buying it.

Analyzing Choose the best answer for each question below.

1   What is the main idea of the passage?
   Ⓐ Many businesses are not able to attract enough customers.
   Ⓑ Business can get more customers by letting them try their products first.
   Ⓒ Some products are too risky to purchase without trying them before buying them.

2   Why are customers not willing to use new products?
   Ⓐ They are more comfortable using products they already know.
   Ⓑ They feel that most businesses do not give out enough samples.
   Ⓒ They only want to purchase products that do not carry any risk.

3   What is the main benefit of giving free samples?
   Ⓐ It helps businesses advertise their products to more customers.
   Ⓑ It allows customers to use a product without spending money on it.
   Ⓒ It prevents customers from becoming too skeptical about a product.

Listening

Listen to a short lecture related to the reading. Take notes on key words and specific information from the lecture.

Notes

Topic	*giving samples to attract*
Detail 1	*DVD shop struggled to make profit; customers*
Detail 2	*owner let customers watch movies for 10 minutes; customers could decide if*
Key Words	*benefits of giving samples; small business became successful;*

02-53

Summarizing Use the chart below to explain the main idea and the key points of the lecture.

Topic	The lecturer explains how businesses can attract more customers by _____ .
Detail 1	He first talks about a DVD shop that _____ to make a profit. Customers would _____ movies but not buy them.
Detail 2	The owner of the store decided to let customers watch the first _____ of movies. This let customers decide if they were _____ in the movies. As a result, the shop's _____ increased.

Synthesizing

Give a brief spoken response to the questions based on the reading passage and the lecture.

1   According to the reading passage, why is it difficult for businesses to attract new customers?

→ *It is difficult for businesses to sell more products because customers* _____ .

2   What problem did the business in lecture have?

→ *The problem the business had is that most of its shoppers did not* _____ .

3   How does the example given by the lecturer prove the argument in the reading passage?

→ *The example proves the argument because it shows how giving samples let a business* _____ .

Speaking

Now give your spoken response for 60 seconds. You may use the guided response to assist you.

? Question

The professor describes how giving samples can improve sales. Explain how the example given by the professor proves this idea.

Guided Response

The passage explains how businesses can sell more products by giving _____ .

The lecturer _____ this idea by giving an example. She talks about a

_____ that had trouble selling its products. Most of its customers would

_____ , but few of them would _____ . So the owner

decided to let shoppers watch the _____ of DVDs. This allowed them to

_____ which DVDs they wanted to buy. The owner's plan worked and allowed

the store to generate more _____ .

Comparing
Listen to a sample response. Then, compare the response with yours.

02-54

skeptical	familiar	overcome	profit	browse
✓	✓	✓	✓	✓

Task 4 Agriculture: Organic Farming

🎯 Vocabulary Take a few moments to review the vocabulary items that will appear in this task.

- **organic** *adj.* being natural rather than manmade
- **pesticide** *n.* poison that kills insects and other similar animals
- **harvest** *v.* to pick crops that are ripe
- **consume** *v.* to eat
- **harm** *v.* to injure or damage in some way

- **fertilizer** *n.* something added to the soil to give it more nutrients
- **manure** *n.* animal excrement that is often added to the soil
- **crop rotation** *n.* the act of changing which crops grow in a field each growing season

Listening

Listen to a lecture on the topic of organic farming. Take notes on key words and concepts in the lecture.

Notes

Topic	*organic farming*
Detail 1	*don't use _____ or _____ ; use natural means to kill insects and weeds*
	no _____ on crops when harvested
	people not _____ by eating them
Detail 2	*no _____ / use _____ ; do _____ ;*
	plant crops good for the soil / _____ the environment
Key Words	*pesticides; weedkiller;*

02-55

Summarizing Using your own words, summarize the topic of the lecture, describe how the professor explains the topic, and restate the key points.

Topic	The topic of the lecture is _____ .
Detail 1	_____ do not use pesticides or weedkillers. Instead, they _____ insects and weeds by using natural means. Their _____ have no chemicals on them when they are _____ . So people are not _____ by eating the crops.
Detail 2	Organic farmers also do not use _____ . They use _____ and crop rotation instead. Some farmers plant crops good for _____ . Those crops put _____ into the soil. As a result, they help improve the _____ .

Speaking

Now give your spoken response for 60 seconds. You may use the guided response to assist you.

? Question

Using points and examples from the lecture, explain two advantages of organic farming.

Guided Response

The professor lectures on _____ . He says it has some _____

_____ . The first is that organic farmers use _____ to kill insects

and weeds. As a result, there are no _____ on their crops when they are

_____ . So people are not hurt by _____ them.

Second, the professor says that organic farmers don't use _____ . Instead, they

use manure and crop rotation. They also plant crops that _____ nutrients to the

soil. In this way, organic farmers help _____ the environment.

Comparing Listen to a sample response. Then compare the response with yours.

02-56

⊛FOCUSING ON PARAPHRASING Read the follow sentences and their paraphrased sentences. Then, practice saying each sentence with natural intonation.

✓ The professor lectures on organic farming.

→ The professor talks to the class about organic farming.

✓ So people are not hurt by eating them.

→ This means that it is safe for people to eat them.

✓ In this way, organic farmers help improve the environment.

→ As a result, organic farmers act to help the environment get better.

Part B

Chapter 08

Independent Speaking

Task 1   Driving Cars vs. Taking Public Transportation

Integrated Speaking

Task 2   Spring Concert Series

Task 3   Psychology: Mental Accounting

Task 4   Animal Science: Electric Fish

Task 1 Driving Cars vs. Taking Public Transportation

Warming Up >> Choose a question at random from the list below. Answer the question right away without making notes. Try to speak for at least 10 seconds.

- How do you prefer to go from place to place? Why? *I prefer to take the bus from place to place. It's convenient and not very expensive.*
- Why do some people prefer to drive cars?
- What are some different types of public transportation?

? Question

Some people prefer to travel by driving cars while others prefer to take public transportation. Talk about the advantages and disadvantages of drive cars or taking public transportation. Use details and examples to explain your answer.

Brainstorming

Choose one of the two opinions you want to speak about. Then, read over the phrases below. Decide which phrases can be used to support your opinion. Finally, choose the correct words to fill out the idea web.

Choice 1 Driving Cars

▶ **Word List**

- no waiting or crowds
- tiring to drive a lot
- go anywhere anytime
- happened to father one time
- don't wait at airport or take crowded buses and trains
- easy to get lost

▶ **Idea Web**

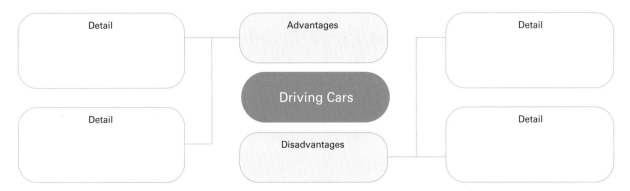

<u>Choice 2</u> **Taking Public Transportation**

▶ **Word List**

- have to walk to some places
- convenient to take
- cheaper than renting a car

- not available everywhere
- get to destinations quickly
- hard to understand bus and subway schedules

▶ **Idea Web**

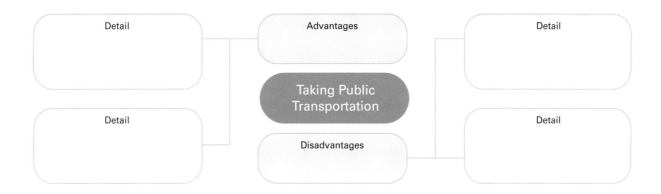

Detail	Advantages	Detail
Detail	**Taking Public Transportation**	Detail
	Disadvantages	

■ Organizing

Look back at the idea web. Use it to organize your response.

My Choice *Driving Cars / Taking Public Transportation*

Advantages

Details

Disadvantages

Details

Speaking

Now give your spoken response for 45 seconds. You may use the guided response to assist you.

Guided Response 1 Driving Cars

There are many advantages to _____ when people travel. One is that they can _____ they want at any time. In addition, travelers who drive do not have to wait _____ for flights at airports. They don't have to take crowded _____ either. However, there are also some _____ to driving cars. It can be _____ to drive from place to place while traveling. Travelers can also easily _____ driving in new cities. This happened to my father once.

Guided Response 2 Taking Public Transportation

I can think of a few _____ of taking public transportation on a trip. First, public transportation is _____. It can get people from _____ quickly. It is also much _____ than renting a car while on a trip. On the other hand, there are some disadvantages. If a traveler is in a _____, it can be difficult to understand the bus or subway _____. And public transportation is not _____ everywhere. So travelers may need to walk at times.

Comparing Listen to a sample response. Then, compare the response with yours.

Driving Cars

Taking Public
Transportation

02-57

02-58

Related Topics

Read the following questions related to the topic. For questions 1 to 3, use the information provided to make responses. For questions 4 and 5, use your own ideas to make responses.

1 What are the advantages and disadvantages of traveling in your home country?

Advantages	Disadvantages
- can travel to places nearby - no cultural or language problems	- not always exciting - may visit same places multiple times

2 What are the advantages and disadvantages of traveling in foreign countries?

Advantages	Disadvantages
- fun and exciting to go to other lands - can see world-famous landmarks	- expensive to visit - may not speak the language well

3 What are the advantages and disadvantages of flying to your destination on a trip?

Advantages	Disadvantages
- can get there fast - easy to get to destination and then back home	- tickets are expensive - flight times can be inconvenient

4 What are the advantages and disadvantages of taking a long trip?

Advantages	Disadvantages

5 What are the advantages and disadvantages of staying at home during vacation?

Advantages	Disadvantages

Task 2 Spring Concert Series

🎯 **Vocabulary** Take a few moments to review the vocabulary items that will appear in this task.

- **council** *n.* a group of people who are chosen to make rules about something
- **local** *adj.* of a particular area, city, or town
- **perform** *v.* to play music or act for other people

- **lawn** *n.* an area of ground covered in short grass
- **admission** *n.* the right to enter a place
- **drawback** *n.* a weakness; a defect

◀ Reading

Read the following announcement from a university.

Spring Concert Series

   This is an announcement from the student council. We are pleased to announce the spring concert series. Come and see your favorite local bands perform their greatest hits. Performances will be held every evening during the month of April on the back lawn of the student center. Admission is free for all current students and $5 for nonstudents. For more information about the concert series, please visit the student council page on the university website.

Analyzing Choose the best answer for each question below.

1   What is the purpose of the announcement?
   (A) To encourage musicians to sign up for a concert
   (B) To advertise a special event for students
   (C) To remind students about the date of a performance

2   Who will be performing during the concert series?
   (A) Musicians from the community
   (B) Student performers
   (C) World-famous bands

3   How much is admission for students currently attending the university?
   (A) Five dollars
   (B) Ten dollars
   (C) No charge

Listening

Listen to a short conversation related to the reading. Take notes about the woman's opinion.

> **Notes**
>
> The woman (agrees / disagrees) with the announcement.
>
> Reason 1 *students are busy; do not have enough time to*
>
> ....
>
> Reason 2 *concerts will be held in main walking area; hard to*
>
> ....
>
> Key Words and Details *students are busy;* ....
>
> ....

02-59

Summarizing Use the chart below to explain the woman's opinion about the announcement.

Main Idea The woman believes the spring concert series has some important ....

....

Reason 1 For one, the woman worries that students are .... to attend
concerts. She says that students have to .... and rest in the
evenings.

Reason 2 The woman then notes that the performances will be held in a ....
If many students attend the concerts, it will be hard to ....
the area. The students will also .... on the lawn.

Synthesizing

Give a brief spoken response to the questions based on the announcement and the conversation.

1 According to the announcement, where will the concerts be held?

   → *The announcement states that the concerts will be held* ....

2 What does the man say in response to the woman's first argument?

   → *He says that students will not be* .... *to attend the concerts.*

3 According to the woman, what is the main problem with the location of concerts?

   → *She says that the concerts will be held in the middle of campus in a main* ....

● Speaking

Now give your spoken response for 60 seconds. You may use the guided response to assist you.

? Question

The woman expresses her opinion of the announcement. Explain her opinion and the reasons she gives for holding it.

Guided Response

The speakers are talking about a _____ at their university. The woman feels

there are some _____ to having concerts on campus. First, the woman

argues that students are _____ to attend concerts. They have to study and

_____ in the evenings. Furthermore, the woman notes that the concerts

will be held in a main _____ . She worries that it will be hard to _____

_____ the area and that the students will _____ on the lawn.

Comparing Listen to a sample response. Then, compare the response with yours.

02-60

⊛‾‾FOCUSING ON STRESS‾ Read the following sentences. Be sure to stress the parts in bold.

✓ We are **pleas**ed to an**noun**ce a **spring** con**cert ser**ies.

✓ The **speak**ers are **talk**ing a**bout** a **spring** con**cert ser**ies at their uni**ver**sity.

✓ For **one**, the **wo**man ar**gues** that **stu**dents are **too busy** to at**tend** con**certs**.

Task 3 Psychology: Mental Accounting

🎯 **Vocabulary** Take a few moments to review the vocabulary items that will appear in this task.

- **mental** *adj.* relating to the mind
- **refer** *v.* to have a connection to something
- **category** *n.* a group of people or things that are similar

- **transfer** *v.* to move from one place to another
- **leftover** *adj.* remaining after something is finished; extra
- **logical** *adj.* sensible; reasonable

◀ Reading

Read the following passage about mental accounting.

Mental Accounting

The term mental accounting refers to the way people think about their money. It describes how people create different categories for money in their minds. They think about the money they have now as well as the money they will have later. The money from one category cannot be transferred to another category. People also give each category different levels of importance. In this way, mental accounting greatly affects how people spend their money.

Analyzing Choose the best answer for each question below.

1 What is the main idea of the passage?
   - Ⓐ Most people categorize their money according to importance.
   - Ⓑ Mental accounting lets people transfer their money to different categories.
   - Ⓒ People place their money into different groups in their minds.

2 Which of the following is true according to the text?
   - Ⓐ Mental accounting causes people to think about the money they will get later.
   - Ⓑ People do not think all types of money have the same importance.
   - Ⓒ Not all people use mental accounting to organize their money.

3 How does mental accounting influence people?
   - Ⓐ It causes people to place their money into different categories.
   - Ⓑ It changes the way that people spend their money.
   - Ⓒ It encourages people to save money instead of spending it.

Listening

Listen to a short lecture related to the reading. Take notes on key words and specific information from the lecture.

> **Notes**
>
> Topic   *the concept of*
>
> Detail 1   *instructor worked at an office; used income to pay*
>
>   02-61
>
> Detail 2   *worked as a waiter on weekends; created different*
>
> Key Words   *worked at an office; paid rent and bills;*

Summarizing Use the chart below to explain the main idea and the key points of the lecture.

> **Topic**   In the listening, the instructor explains the concept of _____ .
>
> **Detail 1**   First, the instructor talks about his experience as an _____ .
> He says that he used the income from this job to pay his _____ .
> He saved the _____ money so that he could buy a house.
>
> **Detail 2**   Next, he says that he had a _____ as a waiter. He explains that
> he used all of the money for _____ . He did this because he
> created a different _____ for his waiter income.

Synthesizing

Give a brief spoken response to the questions based on the reading passage and the lecture.

1   What does the text mention about the money people place in different categories?

→ *It mentions that people do not* _____ *money from one category to another.*

2   How does the instructor explain this concept in the lecture?

→ *He explains that he did not consider using the money from his waiter job to* _____ .

3   What did the instructor do with the money he earned from his waiter job?

→ *He used all of that income only for* _____ .

◀ Speaking

Now give your spoken response for 60 seconds. You may use the guided response to assist you.

? Question

The professor explains mental accounting. Explain the concept and how it is illustrated by the example.

Guided Response

The instructor describes _____ with a personal example. He begins by saying

that he was an _____. He used this income to pay his _____

_____. He used the _____ to save for a house. The instructor

also had a second job as a _____. The income from this job was used

only for _____. He did not _____ using this

money to save for his house. This illustrates the concept in mental accounting that people do not

_____ money across different categories.

Comparing Listen to a sample response. Then, compare the response with yours.

02-62

⚙ FOCUSING ON PRONUNCIATION Practice saying these words by using natural intonation.

category	transfer	logical	consider	quickly
✓	✓	✓	✓	✓

Task 4 Animal Science: Electric Fish

◎ **Vocabulary** Take a few moments to review the vocabulary items that will appear in this task.

- **organ** *n.* a vital part of the body such as the heart or stomach
- **capable** *adj.* able to do
- **generate** *v.* to produce; to make
- **shock** *n.* the effect of a strong charge of electricity
- **volt** *n.* a measure of electrical power

- **territory** *n.* the area where an animal lives
- **navigation** *n.* the act of finding the place one is going to
- **charge** *n.* an amount of electricity
- **detect** *v.* to find something that is hard to see
- **bury** *v.* to hide something in the ground

◀ **Listening**

Listen to a lecture on the topic of electric fish. Take notes on key words and concepts in the lecture.

Notes	
Topic	*how electric fish* _____
Detail 1	_____ *; most of body made up of* _____
	generate very _____ *; used to stun and defend*
	use _____ *for hunting*
Detail 2	_____ *; lives in* _____ *; cannot use sight for* _____
	uses special _____ *in skin to find objects; detect* _____ *of living creatures*
Key Words	*electric organs;* _____

02-63

Summarizing Using your own words, summarize the topic of the lecture, describe how the professor explains the topic, and restate the key points.

Topic The professor explains how _____ use electricity.

Detail 1 For her first example, the professor talks about _____. She explains that electric eels generate _____ to stun other fish and to _____ their territory. However, eels usually use weaker shocks in order to _____.

Detail 2 Next, the professor describes the _____. She says that knife fish uses a _____ in its skin for navigation. This organ _____ the electrical charges given off by _____. With it, the knife fish can find _____ in its environment.

Speaking

Now give your spoken response for 60 seconds. You may use the guided response to assist you.

? Question

Using points and examples from the lecture, explain how electric fish use electricity.

Guided Response

The professor's lecture explains how _____ use electricity. She first talks about the _____ . She explains that most of an eel's body is made up of _____ . It uses these organs to _____ powerful shocks to stun other fish and to _____ its territory. However, it only uses _____ for hunting. Next, the professor talks about _____ . This fish lives in _____ . So it cannot use sight for _____ . Instead, it uses a special organ in its skin to detect _____ given off by living creatures.

Comparing Listen to a sample response. Then, compare the response with yours.

02-64

⊛ **FOCUSING ON PARAPHRASING** Read the follow sentences and their paraphrased sentences. Then, practice saying each sentence with natural intonation.

✓ The professor's lecture explains how electric fish use electricity.

→ In the lecture, the instructor talks about how electric fish use electricity.

✓ It uses these organs to generate powerful shocks to stun other fish and to defend its territory.

→ Eels stun their prey and defend their area by using powerful shocks.

✓ Instead, it uses a special organ in its skin to detect electrical charges given off by living creatures.

→ The knife fish instead uses a special organ in its skin to sense electrical charges made by living creatures.

Part C

Experiencing the TOEFL iBT Actual Tests

Speaking Section Directions

03-01

 Make sure your headset is on.

This section measures your ability to speak about a variety of topics. You will answer four questions by speaking into the microphone. Answer as completely as possible.

In the first question, you will speak about familiar topics. Your response will be scored on your ability to speak clearly and coherently.

In the next two questions, you will first read a short reading passage. This passage will go away, and you will then listen to a talk on the same topic. You will be asked about the information you have read and heard. You will need to combine information from the reading passage and the talk to provide a complete answer. Your response will be scored on your ability to speak clearly and coherently and how accurately you convey information about what you read and heard.

In the last question, you will listen to part of a lecture. You will be asked about what you have heard. Your response will be scored on your ability to speak clearly and coherently and how accurately you convey information about what you heard.

You may take notes while you read and while you listen to the conversations and lectures. You may use your notes to help prepare your response.

Listen carefully to the directions for each question. The directions will not be written on the screen.

For each question, you will be given a short time to prepare your response (15 to 30 seconds, depending on the question). A clock will show how much preparation time is remaining. When the preparation time is up, you will be told to begin your response. A clock will show how much response time is remaining. A message will appear on the screen when the response time has ended.

Task 1

03-02

Do you agree or disagree with the following statement?

Elementary school children should not play computer games.

Include specific details and reasons in your response.

PREPARATION TIME
00:00:15

RESPONSE TIME
00:00:45

Task 2

Poetry Class Cancelation

This is an announcement from the Department of Literature. We regret to inform you that the spring poetry class has been canceled. In recent years, the number of students taking the class has decreased a lot. For this reason, the university has decided to remove the class from the schedule. Students who still wish to take a poetry class may do so at State University. Please talk with your student advisor for more information.

03-03

The man expresses his opinion about the announcement. State his opinion and explain the reasons he gives for holding that opinion.

PREPARATION TIME
00:00:30

RESPONSE TIME
00:00:60

Task 3

The Optimal Foraging Theory

Many animals rely on foraging to obtain their food. Foraging is the act of searching for food. To explain how animals forage for food, ecologists have developed the optimal foraging theory. This theory states that animals work to find foods that are high in calories. At the same time, the animals use the least amount of energy possible while finding their food.

03-04

The professor describes how crows forage for food. Explain how this example illustrates the optimal foraging theory.

PREPARATION TIME
00:00:30

RESPONSE TIME
00:00:60

Task 4

03-05

Using points and examples from the lecture, explain how the Roman Empire was able to expand its territory.

PREPARATION TIME
00:00:20

RESPONSE TIME
00:00:60

CONTINUE   VOLUME

03-06

Speaking Section Directions

 Make sure your headset is on.

This section measures your ability to speak about a variety of topics. You will answer four questions by speaking into the microphone. Answer as completely as possible.

In the first question, you will speak about familiar topics. Your response will be scored on your ability to speak clearly and coherently.

In the next two questions, you will first read a short reading passage. This passage will go away, and you will then listen to a talk on the same topic. You will be asked about the information you have read and heard. You will need to combine information from the reading passage and the talk to provide a complete answer. Your response will be scored on your ability to speak clearly and coherently and how accurately you convey information about what you read and heard.

In the last question, you will listen to part of a lecture. You will be asked about what you have heard. Your response will be scored on your ability to speak clearly and coherently and how accurately you convey information about what you heard.

You may take notes while you read and while you listen to the conversations and lectures. You may use your notes to help prepare your response.

Listen carefully to the directions for each question. The directions will not be written on the screen.

For each question, you will be given a short time to prepare your response (15 to 30 seconds, depending on the question). A clock will show how much preparation time is remaining. When the preparation time is up, you will be told to begin your response. A clock will show how much response time is remaining. A message will appear on the screen when the response time has ended.

Task 1

03-07

Some students prefer to take challenging courses. Other students prefer to take easier classes in order to get high grades. Which of these two opinions do you agree with and why? Include specific details and reasons in your response.

PREPARATION TIME
00:00:15

RESPONSE TIME
00:00:45

Task 2

New Dining Hall to Open

    A new dining hall will open in the fall semester. The dining hall will be located in the basement of Western Hall. There will be 120 seats in the dining hall. The food will be prepared by members of the Department of Hospitality. The dining hall will be similar to a three-star restaurant. As a result, prices there will be higher than those at other dining halls. More information can be found on the school's website.

03-08

The woman gives her opinion of the announcement. State her opinion and explain the reasons she gives for holding that opinion.

PREPARATION TIME
00:00:30

RESPONSE TIME
00:00:60

Task 3

Advertising Strategies

Advertising is a form of communication used to persuade people to buy products or services. To create effective advertisements, advertisers need to utilize advertising strategies. Consequently, advertisers spend a lot of time researching the buying habits of their customers. They also consider the reasons why customers buy certain products. Using this information, advertisers are able to create ads targeted to specific audiences.

03-09

The professor describes milk advertisements. Explain how this example illustrates the concept of advertising strategies.

PREPARATION TIME
00:00:30

RESPONSE TIME
00:00:60

Task 4

03-10

Using points and examples from the lecture, explain how animals become adapted to extreme weather.

PREPARATION TIME
00:00:20

RESPONSE TIME
00:00:60

Appendix

MASTER
WORD LIST

★ MASTER WORD LIST

Chapter 1

- **branch** *n.* a part of a tree that grows out of the trunk

  The tree **branch** has lots of fruit growing on it.

- **conduct** *v.* to carry out; to control

  The military will **conduct** a test of its new weapon.

- **election** *n.* the act of choosing a leader

  The **election** for the president will be held in July.

- **exam** *n.* a test

  The students are nervous about taking the **exam**.

- **gather** *v.* to bring things together into a group; to collect

  Many people like to **gather** at the park on the weekend.

- **get rid of** *exp.* to do away with; to remove

  Please **get rid of** all of the garbage in this room.

- **headline** *n.* the title of a newspaper article

  Many people just read the newspaper **headlines**.

- **include** *v.* to put in a group; to contain

  The registration fee **includes** entrance to all of the speeches at the conference.

- **layer** *n.* one thickness of something over another

  She is wearing several **layers** of clothing to keep warm.

- **margin** *n.* an extra amount

  The profit **margin** for most restaurants is very small.

- **method** *n.* a way of completing a job

  His **method** of solving the problem takes too long.

- **moisture** *n.* wetness

  The **moisture** on the ground in the morning is called dew.

- **period** *n.* a specific length of time during which an event takes place

  There is a waiting **period** of about a week until the results come out.

- **prefer** *v.* to like one thing more than another

  Do you **prefer** to stay in tonight or to go out?

- **produce** *v.* to bring forth; to develop

  The company hopes to **produce** the new medicine before the year ends.

- **protect** *v.* to keep from being damaged or injured; to defend

  The guards will **protect** the people from thieves.

- **reduce** *v.* to make lower in number

  Please try to **reduce** the amount of trash you create.

- **research** *n.* the gathering of information; study

  The scientists are conducting **research** on cancer.

- **root** *n.* the part of a plant that is underground

  The **roots** of some trees can go several meters underground.

- **section** *n.* one of several parts; a piece

  This **section** of the report should be revised.

- **shed** *v.* to fall off; to drop out

  Dogs often **shed** during the spring and summer months.

- **shelf** *n.* a flat, rectangular structure made of wood or metal and used to hold objects

  There are several books sitting on the **shelf**.

- **survey** *n.* a collection of opinions that represents the opinions of many

  The **survey** shows that shoppers prefer domestic clothes to imported ones.

- **survive** *v.* to live

  Many people **survived** the war in their country.

- **trunk** *n.* the main part of a tree

  The **trunk** of that tree is two meters in diameter.

- **upcoming** *adj.* happening in the near future

  That **upcoming** movie looks very exciting.

- **vote** *v.* to decide on a leader

  Who are you going to **vote** for this year?

- **waste** *v.* to use carelessly

  Do not **waste** so much time by watching television.

Chapter 2

- **a great deal** *exp.* very many; several

  There are **a great deal** of fans at the stadium.

- **advantage** *n.* something that helps make another thing better

  There are several **advantages** to working for oneself.

- **attract** *v.* to catch the attention of someone

  He is waving his hands to **attract** the celebrity's attention.

- **campaign** *n.* a series of activities designed to produce a specific result

  The national **campaign** to end littering appears to be working.

- **central** *adj.* main; most important

  The **central** part of the city is the business section.

- **come up with** *phr v.* to think of something

  I cannot **come up with** any new games to play.

- **cooperation** *n.* the act of working together to do something

  It will take a lot of **cooperation** to get the work done.

- **dormitory** *n.* a building on a school campus where students can live

  Lots of university students choose to live in a **dormitory**.

- **effective** *adj.* producing a result that is wanted

  Think of an **effective** solution to the problem.

- **enroll** *v.* to enter as a member or participant

  She hopes to **enroll** at a medical school next year.

- **financial** *adj.* related to money

  Some people have **financial** problems due to bad economic decisions.

- **gain** *v.* to get something that one wants

  The runner in second place is **gaining** on the leader.

- **habit** *n.* a usual way of behaving

  Being lazy is a bad **habit** that people should avoid.

- **income** *n.* money that is earned from work or business

  We hope to increase our **income** by twenty percent this year.

- **incoming** *adj.* arriving at or coming to a place

  We need to take the **incoming** train.

- **influence** *v.* to change something in an indirect way

  Teachers can **influence** the lives of their students.

- **interact** *v.* to talk or do things with others

  She likes to **interact** with all kinds of different people.

- **mating season** *n.* the time of year when animals produce young

  Mating season for many birds is during the spring.

- **particular** *adj.* specific; exact

  Are you looking for something in **particular**?

- **plumage** *n.* feathers that cover the body of a bird

  The **plumage** of the bird of paradise is impressive.

- **policy** *n.* a set of rules or ideas about how to do something

  The company has a new **policy** on the clothes its workers wear.

- **provide** *v.* to make something available; to give

  Please **provide** us with the answer to the problem.

- **purpose** *n.* the reason why something is done or used

  What is the **purpose** of the artwork in the lobby?

- **required** *adj.* needed; essential

  Attendance at the meeting is **required** for everyone.

- **serious** *adj.* having an important or dangerous result

  He has a **serious** illness and needs to see a doctor.

- **shape** *v.* to affect the development of

  The potter **shapes** the clay with his hands to make a pot.

- **species** *n.* a group of animals that are similar

  Throughout history, many **species** of animals have gone extinct.

- **strategy** *n.* a plan used to achieve a goal

  The general has a new **strategy** to win the war.

- **yell** *v.* to say something very loudly

  It is bad manners to **yell** in the library.

Chapter 3

- **assignment** *n.* a job someone has to do

  Please finish this **assignment** no later than Thursday afternoon.

- **check out** *phr v.* to borrow something

  I would like to **check out** these books from the library.

- **construction** *n.* the act of building something

  The **construction** of the tower will take around two years.

- **contribute** *v.* to add to something

  He hopes to **contribute** to society in a positive way.

- **convinced** *adj.* completely sure about something

  I am **convinced** that she is telling the truth.

- **create** *v.* to make something

  Some people are able to **create** all kinds of works of art.

- **crowded** *adj.* filled with people or objects

  The streets are **crowded** with shoppers during the holidays.

- **deteriorate** *v.* to become worse

  Her condition began to **deteriorate** during the past month.

- **development** *n.* the act of making something larger or more advanced

  The **development** of the Internet changed the entire world.

- **efficient** *adj.* able to work without waste

  You can be more **efficient** if you work with your partner.

- **employee** *n.* a worker

  This company has more than 500 **employees**.

- **especially** *adv.* particularly; very

  It is **especially** hot in the tropics during the summer months.

- **exist** *v.* to be real

  Some people believe that ghosts and monsters **exist**.

- **experience** *n.* something that has happened to a person

  He had a positive **experience** when he traveled abroad.

- **flexibility** *n.* the ability to change easily

  He has enough **flexibility** to change his schedule.

- **lesson** *n.* something learned

  He learned a **lesson** about being polite to others.

- **manmade** *adj.* built by human beings; not natural

  The Great Wall of China is an enormous **manmade** structure.

- **purchase** *v.* to buy

  The shopper wants to **purchase** a new car.

- **purpose** *n.* a reason

  The **purpose** of the essay is to convince people to help the environment.

- **quantity** *n.* a number; an amount

  Some people believe **quantity** is better than quality.

- **rapid** *adj.* very fast

  The water is too **rapid** for anyone to swim in it.

- **raw material** *n.* a basic material used to make something

  Oil, gold, and coal are all kinds of **raw materials**.

- **rely on** *phr v.* to need something

  You should not **rely on** a calculator to solve math problems.

- **respect** *v.* to act politely toward others

  It is important to **respect** people older than yourself.

- **run** *v.* to operate; to use something

  His mother **runs** a small bookstore across the street.

- **rural** *adj.* of the countryside and not the city

  Life in **rural** areas is more peaceful than in cities.

- **transport** *v.* to move something from one place to another

Trucks **transport** food and other items all around the country.

- **variety** *n.* a number of different things

  There are a **variety** of performers at the concert tonight.

Chapter 4

- **anchor** *n.* a device that keeps someone or something from moving

  The ship dropped its **anchor** when it arrived in port.

- **bacterial infection** *n.* a disease caused by germs that enter the body

  Take some medicine for that **bacterial infection** you have.

- **blink** *v.* to close and then open one's eyes quickly

  She **blinked** rapidly to get the dirt out of her eyes.

- **breakroom** *n.* an area where people relax

  Several employees are relaxing in the **breakroom** now.

- **compare** *v.* to look at the similarities and differences between two or more things

  Let's **compare** these two animals with each other.

- **consider** *v.* to think about carefully

  Please **consider** several ways to finish the project on time.

- **dust** *n.* very small dry powder

  Please sweep up all of this **dust** in the room.

- **force** *v.* to make someone do something that person does not want to do

  You should not **force** people to spend money they don't have.

- **immune system** *n.* the system that protects one's body from diseases

  Vitamin D can help support the body's **immune system**.

- **impressed** *adj.* feeling deeply or strongly, often in a good way

  We are **impressed** with how well he played the game.

- **joy** *n.* extreme happiness

  He felt nothing but **joy** when he won the marathon.

- **lifetime** *n.* the time during which a person is alive

  The average person lives a **lifetime** of around eighty years.

- **opportunity** *n.* a chance

  He has an **opportunity** to get a new job in London.

- **original** *adj.* relating to the beginning of something

  His **original** idea was very creative.

- **painkiller** *n.* something that reduces pain

  You need to take some **painkillers** after your operation.

- **poor** *adj.* bad; of low quality

  You wrote a **poor** paper and need to rewrite it.

- **protein** *n.* a substance in milk, meat, and other foods that is important for the human diet

  Protein is found in meat and is important to the human body.

- **sophomore** *n.* a student in the second year of high school or college

  The **sophomore** year can be difficult for a lot of students.

- **specialize** *v.* to focus on
  She hopes to **specialize** in robot engineering at college.

- **substance** *n.* a material of a certain type
  The scientists do not know what **substance** is in that asteroid.

- **suffer** *v.* to have a sickness, disease, problem, or something similar
  I do not **suffer** from any illnesses at the moment.

- **suppose** *v.* to believe something to be true
  I **suppose** we should try a different way to fix the machine.

- **topic** *n.* a subject
  She needs to think of a new **topic** for her paper.

- **trust** *v.* to believe
  You have to **trust** the people that you work with.

- **unrealistic** *adj.* not realistic; not possible
  Try not to set **unrealistic** goals for the future.

- **unwind** *v.* to relax
  She likes to **unwind** by watching movies with her friends.

- **various** *adj.* of many different types or kinds
  I have **various** plans for this coming vacation.

Chapter 5

- **apparently** *adv.* seemingly; clearly
  Apparently, it is going to snow a lot this evening.

- **appearance** *n.* the way someone or something looks
  Her **appearance** changed a lot during the summer.

- **budget** *n.* an amount of money that can be spent in a certain period of time
  The department's **budget** stayed the same as last year's.

- **cease** *v.* to stop; to halt
  The rebels were ordered to **cease** fighting the soldiers.

- **constantly** *adv.* at all times; continually
  Earth is **constantly** moving around the sun in space.

- **drastically** *adv.* greatly; very much
  The weather changed **drastically** in just a few hours.

- **edition** *n.* the format in which something is published
  He has a rare first **edition** of that author's book.

- **emotion** *n.* a strong feeling
  What kind of **emotions** did you feel during the race?

- **entirely** *adv.* completely; fully
  I am not **entirely** sure what happened to cause the accident.

- **environment** *n.* the area surrounding something
  The undersea **environment** is full of many mysteries.

- **especially** *adv.* particularly
  She was **especially** pleased when she saw her birthday cake.

- **go out of business** *exp.* to stop doing business
  The store is **going out of business** due to a lack of customers.

- **grab** *v.* to get the attention of somebody

  Let's **grab** his attention by yelling his name loudly.

- **high-pitched** *adj.* making a high sound

  The child still has a very **high-pitched** voice.

- **hunt** *v.* to chase and kill an animal for food

  Lions often **hunt** animals in groups.

- **image** *n.* the thought of how something looks or might look

  The artist created an **image** of what the building would look like.

- **immediately** *adv.* without delay; right away

  You must return to your house **immediately**.

- **ink** *n.* a liquid used for writing and printing

  Please sign your name on the contract in black **ink**.

- **match** *v.* to go well with something

  This hat really **matches** that blue shirt.

- **old fashioned** *adj.* of or relating to the past; outdated

  Some of her ideas are considered a bit **old fashioned**.

- **physical** *adj.* relating to something material

  A person's **physical** power can be improved by lifting weights.

- **print** *v.* to produce by putting written words onto paper

  The paper is **printed** every day of the week.

- **process** *n.* a series of actions that lead to a wanted result

  This is a **process** that must be done exactly in the correct order.

- **reflect** *v.* to bounce back

  A mirror **reflects** light, so that lets people see images.

- **sensitive** *adj.* able to sense very small changes in something

  She is **sensitive** and does not like being criticized by others.

- **version** *n.* a certain form or type of something

  Which **version** of the software is installed on your computer?

Chapter 6

- **athlete** *n.* a person who is good at sports

  She is considered one of her country's best **athletes**.

- **competition** *n.* the act of trying to win something

  At the swimming **competition**, he won three races.

- **compromise** *n.* an agreement in which each group gives up something wanted

  The two sides hope to come to a **compromise** later today.

- **crawl** *v.* to move with the body close to the ground

  The baby learned to **crawl** when he was ten months old.

- **deserted** *adj.* without people; abandoned

  During the war, the city was mostly **deserted** by its residents.

- **dropping** *n.* solid waste from an animal

  There are bird **droppings** all over the sidewalk.

- **enjoyable** *adj.* pleasurable; agreeable

  We had an **enjoyable** evening at the concert last night.

- **fertilizer** *n.* a substance added to soil to help plants grow

  This **fertilizer** should make the soil more productive.

- **fine** *adj.* good; acceptable

  This paper is **fine** and does not need any changes.

- **forthcoming** *adj.* upcoming

  His **forthcoming** novel will be in the fantasy genre.

- **freshman** *n.* a student in the first year of high school or university

  She is currently a **freshman** at the local university.

- **ghost town** *n.* a town that no longer has any people living in it

  There are several **ghost towns** in the American west.

- **introduce** *v.* to bring something to a place for the first time

  Would you please **introduce** me to your father?

- **jealousy** *n.* an unhappy feeling of wanting to have something that somebody else has

  Jealousy is an ugly emotion that people should try not to experience.

- **nutrient** *n.* a substance that plants, animals, and people need to live and grow

  There are not enough **nutrients** in junk food.

- **organic** *adj.* of living things

  Organic farming methods have become common in some places.

- **orientation** *n.* the time when new students are introduced to their school

  Orientation at some colleges can last for a couple of days.

- **peace** *n.* a time without fighting

  There were ten years of **peace** before fighting started again.

- **pest** *n.* an animal that damages plants

  Farmers try to kill **pests** that eat their crops.

- **recognize** *v.* to give special attention

  Are you able to **recognize** anyone in this picture?

- **severe** *adj.* very bad, serious, or unpleasant

  She has a **severe** neck injury so will be taken to the hospital.

- **topsoil** *n.* the upper layer of dirt

  The **topsoil** needs more water to help the plants grow.

- **transition** *n.* a change from one condition to another

  The **transition** to the business world can be difficult for some people.

- **unique** *adj.* belonging to only one person; one of a kind

  He came up with **unique** ideas all the time.

- **vice versa** *adv.* in reverse order from what is stated; conversely

  I really like him, and **vice versa**.

Chapter 7

- **apologize** *v.* to say that one is sorry for doing something wrong

  You had better **apologize** because you made him upset.

- **browse** *v.* to look at many things in a store to find something worth buying

  I enjoy going to the store just to **browse** the shelves.

- **consume** *v.* to eat
  She tries to **consume** lots of protein every day.

- **continually** *adv.* happening all the time
  She is **continually** looking for a new job.

- **crop rotation** *n.* the act of changing which crops grow in a field each growing season
  Crop rotation was commonly used in the Middle Ages.

- **enlarge** *v.* to make something bigger
  Is it possible to **enlarge** some of the rooms in the house?

- **expose** *v.* to cause to be visible; to show
  The wind blew away the sand and **exposed** the ruins of the city.

- **fertilizer** *n.* something added to the soil to give it more nutrients
  There is not enough **fertilizer** in the soil.

- **harm** *v.* to injure or damage in some way
  You should not **harm** innocent animals.

- **harvest** *v.* to pick crops that are ripe
  They are going to **harvest** the corn in the fields.

- **inconvenience** *n.* trouble; problems
  We are really sorry about the **inconvenience** we caused.

- **manure** *n.* animal excrement that is often added to the soil
  Be careful that you do not step in that cow **manure**.

- **organic** *adj.* being natural rather than manmade
  Organic crops can be very expensive at supermarkets.

- **overcome** *v.* to defeat someone or something
  If you try hard enough, you can **overcome** all obstacles.

- **pesticide** *n.* poison that kills insects and other similar animals
  Try not to use too much **pesticide** on the crops.

- **profit** *n.* money made by a business
  There is not a lot of **profit** in the restaurant industry.

- **realize** *v.* to come to believe; to recognize
  He suddenly **realized** that he was able to play well.

- **renovate** *v.* to make changes and repairs to an old building so that it is in good condition
  They plan to **renovate** their home this summer.

- **risk** *n.* the possibility that something bad will happen
  There is the **risk** of death if you have the operation.

- **skeptical** *adj.* having doubt about a statement
  I am a bit **skeptical** about the advice you gave me.

- **struggle** *v.* to try very hard to deal with something difficult
  He **struggles** to understand why people act badly sometimes.

- **take** *v.* to think about; to consider
  I need to **take** some time before I make a decision.

- **work out** *phr v.* to exercise
  She likes to **work out** at the gym five days a week.

Chapter 8

- **admission** *n.* the right to enter a place
  The price of **admission** to the museum is five dollars.

- **bury** *v.* to hide something in the ground
  Some animals like to **bury** extra food underground.

- **capable** *adj.* able to do
  Robots are **capable** of doing more work than humans.

- **category** *n.* a group of people or things that are similar
  This work belongs in the fiction **category**.

- **charge** *n.* an amount of electricity
  There is only a small **charge** of energy left.

- **council** *n.* a group of people who are chosen to make rules about something
  The city **council** will vote on the matter tonight.

- **detect** *n.* to find something that is hard to see
  Let's look at the engine and **detect** the problem.

- **drawback** *n.* a weakness; a defect
  Please think of some **drawbacks** to signing this contract.

- **generate** *v.* to produce; to make
  The dam can **generate** enough electricity for the entire city.

- **lawn** *n.* an area of ground covered in short grass
  It takes a lot of effort to make the **lawn** look nice.

- **leftover** *adj.* remaining after something is finished; extra
  There is some **leftover** food in the refrigerator.

- **local** *adj.* of a particular area, city, or town
  The **local** government is not listening to its residents.

- **logical** *adj.* sensible; reasonable
  Your solution to the problem is quite **logical**.

- **mental** *adj.* relating to the mind
  Mental exercise is just as important as physical exercise.

- **navigation** *n.* the act of finding the place one is going to
  The art of **navigation** on the ocean can take time to learn.

- **organ** *n.* a vital part of the body such as the heart or stomach
  The heart and the brain are two important **organs**.

- **perform** *v.* to play music or act for other people
  She will **perform** her hit song later in the concert.

- **refer** *v.* to have a connection to something
  Please **refer** to the guidebook if you have any questions.

- **shock** *n.* the effect of a strong charge of electricity
  He felt a sudden **shock** when he touched the wire.

- **territory** *n.* the area where an animal lives
  The country lost some **territory** at the end of the war.

- **transfer** *v.* to move from one place to another
  You need to **transfer** to the blue line at the next stop.

- **volt** *n.* a measure of electrical power
  How many **volts** of electricity are in this battery?

MEMO

MEMO

MEMO

TOEFL MAP Speaking

New TOEFL Edition

Basic

Scripts and Answer Key

 **DARAKWON**

TOEFL® MAP Speaking

New TOEFL® Edition

Basic

Scripts and Answer Key

DARAKWON

Part B

● Chapter | **01** Independent Speaking

Task 1 Children Should Receive Money for Chores

■ Brainstorming
p.26

Choice 1 Receive Money

Reason 1: encourages children to work well

Details: children do not like doing chores;
money is a reason to work hard

Reason 2: also teaches about rewards

Details: learn that work is rewarded with money;
important concept in life

Choice 2 Not Receive Money

Reason 1: learn about responsibility

Details: family must work together;
everybody should help out

Reason 2: paying for chores is also unequal

Details: parents get no pay for chores;
children should not get special treatment

■ Organizing

Answers may vary.

My Choice: *Receive Money*

First Reason: *can motivate children to work hard*

Details: *not many children like doing chores; money
gives them a reason to complete their tasks*

Second Reason: *also learn about the idea of
rewards*

Details: *learn that doing work earns money;
important concept in life*

My Choice: *Not Receive Money*

First Reason: *children must learn that chores are a
family responsibility*

Details: *all family members must work together to
take care of their home*

Second Reason: *paying children is unequal*

Details: *parents do not receive pay for chores;
children should not be treated differently*

■ Speaking
p.28

Guided Response 1 Receive Money   02-01

I agree that children should *receive money* for doing
household chores. For one, giving money to children
for doing chores can *motivate* them to work hard. Not
many children like *doing chores*. So paying children
gives them a reason to *complete* all their tasks. Children
can also learn about the idea of *rewards*. Children learn
that doing work allows them to *earn money*. This is a
very *important concept* in life, so it is important to teach
children about it early.

Guided Response 2 Not Receive Money   02-02

To me, parents should not have to *give* their children
money for doing chores. First of all, children must learn
that chores are a *family responsibility*. They need to
understand that members of a family all *work together*
to care for their home. What's more, paying children for
chores is *unequal*. Parents do chores around the home
but do not receive *any pay*. Therefore, children should
not receive *special treatment* when it comes to doing
chores.

■ Related Topics
p.29

Sample Response

Answers may vary.

4

Agree	Disagree
• *make their children tired* • *children become angry at parents*	• *most chores are easy to do* • *teaches children responsibility*

5

Agree	Disagree
• *need to focus on schoolwork* • *let children relax more*	• *one or two hours of chores is not much* • *some households have many chores to do → parents need help*

Task 2 Library to Reduce Book Collection

■ Reading   p.30

Analyzing

1 (B)

2 (B)

3 (C)

■ Listening   p.31

`Script & Notes` 02-03

M: I read in the paper that the university library is going to get rid of many of its books. Personally, I think this is a terrible idea.

W: Really? Why is that?

M: I like having a huge selection of books available. That has helped me study for my classes.

W: I have to completely disagree with you. Getting rid of the books that nobody ever uses is a smart move. They are just wasting space in the library. The space could be used to create new study areas for students.

M: But if they get rid of the books, how can students do research?

W: These days, most students prefer to do their research on the Internet. By making the computer center larger, more students will be able to do their schoolwork during busy times.

M: That's a good point. Maybe getting rid of the books is not such a bad idea after all.

> *Notes*
>
> The woman **agrees** with the announcement.
>
> **Reason:** *books wasting space; most students do research online*
>
> **Key Words and Details:** *smart move; wasting space; prefer to do research on Internet; more students do schoolwork during busy times*

Summarizing

Main Idea

The woman feels that the university's plan is a *smart move.*

Reason 1

She believes that the books are *wasting space* in the

library. The space could be used to make new *study areas* for students.

Reason 2

She also mentions that most students *prefer* doing their research online. By making the computer center *larger*, more students will be able to do their *schoolwork* during busy times.

Synthesizing

1 The man feels that the plan *is a terrible idea.*

2 The woman feels differently than the man by saying that the plan is a *smart move.*

3 Students can benefit because the computer center *will be made larger.*

■ Speaking   p.32

Guided Response   02-04

The man and the woman are talking about the university's plans to get rid of *several of its books*. The woman *agrees* with the plan. She explains that the books not used by students simply *waste space* in the library. She feels that the library could use this space to create new *study areas* for students. The woman also mentions that most students choose to do their research *online*. Furthermore, the woman believes that more students will be able to do their schoolwork during *busy times* if the computer lab is *made larger*.

Task 3 Statistics: Sampling Bias

■ Reading   p.33

Analyzing

1 (C)

2 (B)

3 (B)

■ Listening   p.34

`Script & Notes` 02-05

Professor: Now, I want to tell you how sampling bias led to one embarrassing news story about the 1948 presidential election.

On the night of the election, one newspaper wrote on its front page that Thomas Dewey had defeated President Truman in the election. The newspaper wrote this story before the votes were counted. How did the newspaper come up with this headline? It conducted a survey. The problem with the survey was that it was only done over the telephone. Back then, only rich people had telephones . . . And rich people were more likely to vote for Dewey. But most people actually wanted to vote for Truman. Since they did not have telephones, they were not included in the survey. Because of this, the survey was completely wrong. President Truman won the election over Dewey by a huge margin.

> **Notes**
>
> **Topic:** *1948 presidential election*
>
> **Detail 1:** *newspaper story: Dewey defeated Truman headline made from survey*
>
> **Detail 2:** *only rich people had telephones survey results completely wrong*
>
> **Key Words:** *before votes were counted; only done over phone; rich people; survey completely wrong*

Summarizing

Topic

The main idea of the lecture is the *1948 presidential election*.

Detail 1

The professor explains that one newspaper incorrectly wrote that Dewey *had defeated Truman* in the election. The newspaper wrote this story based on a *survey*.

Detail 2

The survey was done *over the telephone*, so it only included rich people. These people were more likely to *vote for Dewey*. Therefore, the survey results were *completely incorrect*.

Synthesizing

1   The main problem with sampling bias is that it produces *inaccurate results*.

2   The survey method talked about in the lecture was *a telephone survey*.

3   This method affected the results by including only *rich people*.

■ Speaking
p.35

Guided Response 02-06

The topic of the reading passage is *sampling bias*. This is when a survey does not include *all of the members* of a group. It usually creates *incorrect results*. To explain sampling bias, the professor talks about the 1948 *presidential election*. He explains that one newspaper said that Thomas Dewey *had defeated* President Truman in the election. This *headline* was based on a survey. The survey was done *over the telephone*, so only *rich people* were included. Consequently, the result of the survey was *completely wrong*.

● Chapter | **01** Integrated Speaking

Task 4 Plant Biology: Trees Shedding Leaves

■ Listening
p.36

Script & Notes 02-07

Professor: Have you ever wondered why some trees shed their leaves during the winter? This occurs for many reasons, but the main reason trees do this is to protect themselves.

You know, most trees that lose their leaves are in cold climates. During the long, cold winters, the air in these places becomes very dry. This causes the leaves of trees also to become dry. To keep the leaves alive, the trees have to give them a lot of moisture. The problem with this is that the trees could lose too much moisture and die. So instead of giving moisture to the leaves, the trees keep the moisture inside . . . They keep it in their trunks and branches. After a while, the leaves start to die. As the leaves die, they fall to the ground around the trees. When this happens, the leaves actually help the trees survive. How, you may ask? Well, the leaves form a protective layer around the roots of the trees. This allows the roots to stay warm. So by losing their leaves, the trees are able to live through the winter.

> **Notes**
>
> **Topic:** *trees shedding leaves; done to protect themselves*
>
> **Detail 1:** *live in cold climates; leaves use a lot of moisture*
> *keeping leaves alive causes trees to lose moisture*
>
> **Detail 2:** *leaves start to die; fall to the ground form a protective layer*

Key Words: *cold climates; air becomes dry; moisture; protective layer*

Summarizing

Topic

In the lecture, the professor explains why trees *shed their leaves*. She claims that trees do this to protect themselves.

Detail 1

During the winter, the leaves need a lot of *moisture*. If the trees give moisture to the leaves, they might *die*. So they keep moisture inside their trunks and *branches*.

Detail 2

The leaves die and fall *to the ground*. This creates a *layer* that protects the roots of the trees.

■ Speaking   p.37

Guided Response   02-08

The lecture mainly discusses why trees *lose their leaves* during winter. According to the speaker, trees do this to *protect themselves*. During the winter, trees use a lot of *moisture* to keep their leaves alive. If the trees lose too much moisture, they can *die*. So they keep their moisture inside their trunks and *branches*. This causes *the leaves* to die. As they fall to the ground, they form a *protective layer* over the roots of the trees. Together, these factors allow the trees to live *through the winter*.

● Chapter | **02 Independent Writing**

Task 1 Deciding on a Teacher to Hire

■ Brainstorming   p.40

Choice 1 Hire an Arts and Crafts Teacher

Reason 1: can do fun activities

Details: classes not always interesting;
enjoy making things during class

Reason 2: become more creative

Details: come up with unique designs;
be proud of their new ideas

Choice 2 Hire a Computer Programming Teacher

Reason 1: computers important in society

Details: use to work, play, and study;
understand computers better

Reason 2: jobs require programming skills

Details: get valuable experience;
help get a job in the future

■ Organizing

Answers may vary.

My Choice: *Hire an Arts and Crafts Teacher*

First Reason: *can do fun activities in class*

Details: *most classes aren't fun; but can enjoy making things in arts and crafts classes*

Second Reason: *learn to become more creative*

Details: *come up with unique designs; be proud of the new ideas they think of*

My Choice: *Hire a Computer Programming Teacher*

First Reason: *computers important to society*

Details: *use computers for working, playing, and studying; learn to understand computers better*

Second Reason: *many jobs need programming skills*

Details: *can get experience; will help students find jobs later*

■ Speaking   p.42

Guided Response 1 Hire an Arts and Crafts Teacher   02-09

In my opinion, the school *ought to* hire an arts and crafts teacher. First, arts and crafts are *fun and exciting* activities for students. Many school classes are pretty *boring* for students. But they will have *plenty* of fun making things during their arts and crafts classes. In addition, the teacher can help the students become *more creative*. For instance, they can think of *unique designs* to make. After making things, they will be proud since it will show their *imaginations*.

Guided Response 2 Hire a Computer Programming Teacher   02-10

Of the three choices, the best one is to *hire* a computer programming teacher. To begin with, computers are an extremely important part of *society* now. People use computers to work, *play*, and study. A computer programming teacher can *assist* students in understanding computers better. Secondly, many jobs require workers to have computer programming *skills*.

If students learn programming, they can get *valuable* experience. That will help them get good jobs that pay lots of *money* after graduation.

Related Topics

p.43

Sample Response

Answers may vary.

4

Agree	Disagree
• *many facilities in poor condition → need repairing* • *lots of schools lack certain facilities → not fair to students*	• *schools waste lots of money on unnecessary facilities* • *comes from tax money → have to raise taxes on residents*

5

A Gymnasium	A Library
• *let students have fun playing sports* • *get students in good physical shape*	• *improve the minds of students* • *provide quiet place for studying*

● Chapter | **02** Integrated Speaking

Task 2 University Housing Policy Change

Reading

p.44

Analyzing

1 Ⓐ

2 Ⓒ

3 Ⓑ

Listening

p.45

Script & Notes 02-11

W: Did you receive that email about the housing problem from the school president?

M: Yes, I read it this morning.

W: I didn't realize the school's financial problems were so serious. But it seems that this plan is the best way to solve the problem.

M: I'm not so sure of that.

W: What do you mean?

M: Well, not all of the incoming students will want to live in the dorms. They might want to live with their parents and save money. If that's the case, then these students will not enroll at our university. Then there won't be enough new students for the school's plan to work.

W: I see what you're saying. How can the school solve its financial problems then?

M: I think the school should lower the price to stay in the dorms. Housing fees are too expensive. That's why the older students moved out. If the school makes the dorms less expensive, then more students will live in them.

Notes

The man ***disagrees*** with the announcement.

Reason: *incoming students may not want to live in dorms; may not enroll at university, so school's policy will not work*

Key Words and Details: *financial problems; incoming students; want to save money; will not enroll at university; dorms too expensive*

Summarizing

Main Idea

In the man's opinion, the school's plan may not be the *best way* to solve the problem.

Reason 1

He worries that not all of the *incoming students* will want to live in the dorms. Therefore, they might not *enroll* at the university. If that happens, then the school will not make *enough money*.

Reason 2

The man also feels that housing fees are *too expensive*. By making the dorms *cheaper*, more students will *live* in them.

Synthesizing

1 The man disagrees with the woman. He is not sure that the plan *will work well*.

2 The university wants freshmen to live in the dorms in order to make up for the school's *reduced income*.

3 He feels this way because many incoming students will not want to *live in the dorms*.

Speaking

p.46

Guided Response

02-12

The speakers are discussing the university's *housing policy* change. The woman thinks the plan is a good idea. However, the man is *not sure* it will work. His first concern is that many incoming students will not want to live in the *dorms*. So they will not enroll in the university. If this happens, then the university's plan will *not work*. Therefore, the man thinks that the school should make the dorms *less expensive*. Then, more students will choose to *live* in them.

● Chapter | 02 Integrated Speaking

Task 3 Business: Promotions

Reading

p.47

Analyzing

1 Ⓐ

2 Ⓑ

3 Ⓐ

Listening

p.48

Script & Notes 02-13

Professor: All right, so we know that businesses have several ways to shape their customers' buying habits. Today, I want to talk about one particular strategy: promotions. You see, good promotions are essential for the success of a business. Let me illustrate this with an example.

I have a friend who owns a restaurant. His restaurant is quite successful. He always has a lot of customers during dinnertime. In fact, customers usually have to wait in line just to be seated. But he had a problem. His restaurant never had any customers before dinnertime. To solve this problem, my friend came up with a promotion. He created an early-bird dinner special. Can you guess what happened? That's right. He was able to attract many customers during the late afternoon with his promotion.

As you can see, promotions help a business make more money by bringing in more customers.

Notes

Topic: *business promotions*

Detail 1: *friend owns restaurant; successful; many customers during dinner but no customers before dinnertime*

Detail 2: *came up with a promotion attracted many customers before dinner*

Key Words: *promotions essential for success; early-bird dinner special*

Summarizing

Topic

The main topic of the discussion is *business promotions*.

Detail 1

The lecturer first talks about a friend who *owns a restaurant*. His friend always has a lot of customers *during dinnertime*. However, the friend did not have many customers *before dinnertime*.

Detail 2

To solve this problem, the friend created a *promotion*. This *attracted* many customers to the restaurant before dinnertime. In this way, businesses can *bring in* more customers and make *more money*.

Synthesizing

1 Promotions help businesses make more money by *attracting more customers*.

2 He talked about an early-bird special, which is a *special promotion*.

3 The promotion discussed in the lecture attracted *many customers* to the restaurant before dinnertime.

Speaking

p.49

Guided Response

02-14

The reading passage states that businesses use promotions to attract more customers and to generate *more income*. The lecturer explains this idea by mentioning his friend's *restaurant*. The restaurant always has *many customers* during dinnertime. However, it did not have many customers *before dinner*. To solve this problem, the lecturer's friend created an early-bird *dinner special* promotion. The plan attracted many customers to the restaurant *before* dinnertime. So the promotion was a *success*. This example shows how promotions can *bring in* more customers and make *more money*.

Task 4 Animal Science: Display Behavior

■ Listening
p.50

Script & Notes 02-15

Professor: Now I want to tell you a little bit about animal behavior. Animals use something called display behavior to interact with other members of their species. To explain, I'll talk about two animals known for their display behavior: the monkey and the peacock.

We've all seen monkeys at the zoo yelling, seemingly for no reason. But this is actually display behavior. You see, monkeys yell at other monkeys to gain advantages. Here, I'll explain. Suppose a monkey has found food. Another monkey sees the food and wants it as well. In this case, the second monkey will give a warning yell. This scares the first monkey away from the food. By using display behavior, the second monkey is able to get a meal.

Perhaps the most famous example of display behavior comes from peacocks. Male peacocks are well known for their beautiful plumage. It is beautiful to look at, but it serves another purpose. Any idea what this could be? Yes, exactly. It attracts female peacocks. During mating season, male peacocks walk around to show off their plumage. Those with the most beautiful plumage can attract the most females. So this behavior does not mean much for other animals. But it is a central behavior in peacock mating.

Notes

Topic: *animals use display behavior to interact with other members of their species*

Detail 1: *monkeys yell at other monkeys; do this to gain advantages; give warning yells*

Detail 2: *male peacocks have plumage; use this to attract females; show off plumage during mating season*

Key Words: *display behavior; monkeys yell; gain advantages; peacocks plumage; attract females*

Summarizing

Topic

The instructor discusses *display behavior*. She illustrates this by talking about *monkeys* and *peacocks*.

Detail 1

Monkeys *yell* at one another as display behavior. If one monkey finds food, another monkey will give out a *warning yell*. This yell *scares* the first monkey away from the food.

Detail 2

Male peacocks have *beautiful plumage*. The purpose of it is to *attract females*. Male peacocks show off their plumage during *mating season*. Those with the *best plumage* attract the most females.

■ Speaking
p.51

Guided Response
02-16

In the lecture, the instructor talks about the *display behavior* of animals. She *illustrates* this by mentioning the display behavior of monkeys and peacocks. First, the instructor claims that monkeys *yell* at one another as a form of display behavior. If one monkey gets food, another monkey will give a *warning yell*. This scares the first monkey *away* from the food. The instructor then talks about the plumage of *male peacocks*. She explains that male peacocks use their *plumage* to attract females. Those with the best plumage attract the *most females*.

● Chapter | 03 Independent Writing

Task 1 Taking Notes in Class vs. Concentrating on Lectures

■ Brainstorming
p.54

Choice 1 Taking Notes

Reason 1: make it easier to study

Details: easily review class material; cannot remember the entire lecture

Reason 2: lets teacher know I am paying attention

Details: many classes have participation grades; teacher thinks do not care about class

Choice 2 Concentrating on Lectures

Reason 1: taking notes distracting

Details: can focus on the material; think about the lecture

Reason 2: participate more easily as well

Details: ask the teacher questions;
share my own ideas in class

Organizing

Answers may vary.

> **My Choice:** *Taking Notes*
>
> **First Reason:** *lets me study more easily*
>
> **Details:** *easily go over the class lecture; cannot remember every detail*
>
> **Second Reason:** *also shows the teacher you are paying attention*
>
> **Details:** *many classes have participation grades; the teacher thinks do not care about class*

> **My Choice:** *Concentrating on the Lectures*
>
> **First Reason:** *note-taking distracts me*
>
> **Details:** *can focus on the material*
>
> **Second Reason:** *also able to participate more easily*
>
> **Details:** *ask the teacher questions; share my own ideas in class*

Speaking

p.56

Guided Response 1 Taking Notes

02-17

I prefer *taking notes* in class rather than just concentrating on the lectures. To begin with, notes make it *easier to study*. I can easily look at my notes to *review* the material covered in my classes. After all, it's almost impossible to remember *every part* of a lecture. Furthermore, taking notes shows the teacher that I'm *paying attention*. This is especially important because many classes have *participation grades*. If I sit in class without taking notes, the teacher will think I *don't care* about the class.

Guided Response 2 Concentrating on Lectures

02-18

Most students take notes in class. As for me, I am convinced that *concentrating* on lectures is better. One reason is that I *can focus* on the material. When I take notes, I get *distracted*. By focusing only on lectures, I *can understand* the material better. Concentrating on lectures also allows me to *participate* more easily. I can *think about* the lectures and *ask* the teacher questions. This way, I can remember the material *long term*, so I don't have to study as much outside class.

Related Topics

p.57

Sample Response

Answers may vary.

4

No Homework	A Lot of Homework
• is usually just busy work • lets students have free time after school	• need to practice to learn material better • can help students figure out what they do and don't know

5

Agree	Disagree
• more important for technological society • harder subjects to learn so should teach more classes	• should teach all subjects equal amounts • liberal arts classes are still important

● Chapter | 03 Integrated Speaking

Task 2 Loaning Laptops to Students

Reading

p.58

Analyzing

1 (A)

2 (C)

3 (B)

Listening

p.59

Script & Notes 02-19

W: What do you think about the school's plan to loan laptops to students?

M: In all honesty, I'm not convinced that the plan will be successful.

W: Yeah, I feel the same way. I think the school should use the money for other things.

M: Oh, for sure. Like the desktop computers in the computer labs. Most of them are really old and need to be updated.

W: Yeah, I once tried to do an assignment for a design class in a computer lab. But I couldn't because the computers were too old to run the program I needed.

M: Exactly. I'm also worried that the service in the computer labs will deteriorate. There will probably be a lot of students checking out these laptops. So the staff probably won't have time to answer questions or to help students if they have any problems.

W: I hear you. I just hope the school will reconsider its plan before it's too late.

> **Notes**
>
> The man **disagrees** with the school's decision.
>
> **Reason:** *school needs to purchase new computers for labs; woman could not do assignment; service in computer labs will deteriorate*
>
> **Key Words and Details:** *most computers really old; computers could not run program; a lot of students check out computers; no time to answer questions or help students*

Summarizing

Main Idea

The man in the conversation is *not convinced* that his school's plan to loan laptops to students will be successful.

Reason 1

For his first argument, the man states that the school needs to buy *new computers* for the computer labs. He says that most of the computers in the labs are *really old*.

Reason 2

The man also worries that the service in the computer labs will *deteriorate*. He feels the employees will be *too busy* to answer questions or to help students with computer problems.

Synthesizing

1 The university hopes to *make the computer labs less crowded*.

2 He says that the computers are *really old*.

3 The man says that the workers will be too busy checking out laptops to *answer questions and to help students with problems*.

■ Speaking
p.60

Guided Response
02-20

The speakers are discussing their school's decision to allow students to *borrow laptops*. The man is *not*

---

convinced the plan will work. The man gives *two arguments* to explain his opinion. His first argument is that the computers in the labs are *too old*. The man believes the school should buy *some new computers* instead of laptops. He is also worried that the service in the computer labs will *deteriorate*. He thinks the staff will be too busy renting laptops to *help students* using the labs.

● Chapter | **03** Integrated Speaking

Task 3 Education: Teaching Students to Follow the Rules

■ Reading
p.61

Analyzing

1 Ⓑ

2 Ⓒ

3 Ⓐ

■ Listening
p.62

Script & Notes 02-21

Professor: Let me tell you about my experience as an elementary school teacher and how I taught students to follow the rules.

If you've ever been around young children, then you know that they love to ask why. This is especially true of rules. Young students need to know why a rule exists. Otherwise, they won't follow it. This means you should always explain the purpose of a rule after making it. I'll give you an example to help you understand. I didn't want my students to eat snacks in the classroom. So I made a rule against eating in class. At first, the students didn't follow the rule. But then I explained why I made the rule. I told them that I wanted to keep the classroom clean. Once the students understood the purpose of the rule, they followed it without a problem.

> **Notes**
>
> **Topic:** *teaching students to follow the rules*
>
> **Detail 1:** *young students need to know why a rule exists; otherwise will not follow it teachers must explain purpose of rule*
>
> **Detail 2:** *teacher did not want students eating in class; students did not follow rule at first; after explaining why made rule, students followed it without problem*

Key Words: *experience as elementary school teacher; young children ask why; need to know why rule exists*

Summarizing

Topic

The lecturer explains how she taught her elementary students to *follow the rules*.

Detail 1

First, she explains that young children love to *ask why*. She says that young students need to know the *purpose* of a rule. Otherwise, they will *not follow* the rule.

Detail 2

The lecturer made a rule against *eating in class*. The students did not follow the rule *at first*. However, after she *explained* the purpose of the rule, the students *followed it* without a problem.

Synthesizing

1   The passage says that it is difficult and that teachers must rely on *a variety of strategies to do so*.

2   She created a rule against *eating snacks in class*.

3   The instructor would *explain the purpose* of the rules to get her students to follow them.

■ Speaking   p.63

Guided Response   02-22

The reading passage deals with *teaching rules* to students. It explains that teachers must use a variety of *strategies* to teach students the rules. In the listening, the lecturer claims that *young children* will not follow a rule if they don't know why it *exists*. She gives an example to explain. The lecturer made a rule against *eating in class*. At first, the students *didn't follow* the rule. But after she explained the *purpose* of the rule, the students followed it *without a problem*.

● Chapter | 03 **Integrated Speaking**

Task 4 **History: The American Industrial Revolution**

■ Listening   p.64

Professor: At the beginning of the nineteenth century, the United States went through a time of rapid development known as the Industrial Revolution. Several factors contributed to the revolution. Today, however, I'll just focus on the development of water and land transportation systems.

Before the Industrial Revolution, the only way to travel around the U.S. was on foot or horseback. As you can guess, this was not very efficient. So the country began the construction of canals. These manmade waterways made it possible to transport goods from the ocean to places as far away as Chicago with ease. One result of this was lower prices on goods and services.

Of course, canals could not be built everywhere. The nation needed a way to connect areas far from water with the rest of the country. Enter the railway systems. Trains could move even larger quantities of goods than canals. They also made it possible to send raw materials from the rural South directly to the North. In this way, railway systems lowered the cost of transporting goods even further. This, in turn, created more industrial development.

Notes

Topic: *American Industrial Revolution; development of water and land transportation systems*

Detail 1: *before IR, only traveled on foot or horseback; construction of canals*
made it possible to transport goods to places far from ocean

Detail 2: *canals could not be built far from water; construction of railroads*
moved larger quantities of goods than canals; transported goods from rural South to North

Key Words: *water and land transportation; not efficient; manmade waterways; raw materials; lower transportation costs*

Summarizing

Topic

The speaker goes over the development of *water and land transportation* during the American Industrial Revolution.

Detail 1

The country built *canals* to transport goods to places far from the *ocean*. This resulted in *lower prices* on goods and services.

Detail 2

Canals could not be built *everywhere*. So the nation built *railroads*. Trains could move *larger quantities* of goods than canals. They also made it possible to send *raw materials* directly to the North.

■ Speaking
p.65

Guided Response
02-24

The speaker goes over the development of *water and land transportation* during the American Industrial Revolution. Originally, people did not have an *efficient* way to travel around the U.S., so the nation constructed *canals*. These made it possible to *transport* goods to places far from the *ocean* cheaply. Later, the nation constructed *railroads*. Railroad trains could move *more goods* than canals. They also made it possible to transport *raw materials* easily from the South to the North. This lowered *transportation costs* further, allowing the U.S. to become more developed.

● Chapter | 04 Independent Writing

Task 1 Educational Programs vs. Entertainment Programs

■ Brainstorming
p.68

Choice 1 Educational Programs

Reason 1: learn valuable information

Details: how to escape a burning building; how to save someone's life

Reason 2: also cover a variety of topics

Details: shows on science and history; programs about engineering

Choice 2 Entertainment Programs

Reason 1: want to relax

Details: clear my head of problems; not worry about the real world

Reason 2: can also improve my mood

Details: watching comedy programs; help relieve stress

■ Organizing

Answers may vary.

> **My Choice:** *Educational Programs*
>
> **First Reason:** *learn valuable information*
>
> **Details:** *one program taught me how to escape from a burning building*
>
> **Second Reason:** *also cover a variety of topics*
>
> **Details:** *shows about science, history, and engineering*

> **My Choice:** *Entertainment Programs*
>
> **First Reason:** *want to relax when watching television*
>
> **Details:** *clear my head; do not have to worry about the world and its problems*
>
> **Second Reason:** *can also improve my mood*
>
> **Details:** *watching comedy programs makes me happier and less stressed*

■ Speaking
p.70

Guided Response 1 Educational Programs
02-25

When I watch television, I mostly watch *educational programs*. There are two reasons I feel this way. First, I can learn *valuable information* from these programs. For instance, one program taught me how to escape from a *burning building*. I also prefer educational programs because they cover a *variety of topics*. Many *different types* of educational programs exist. These include programs about science, history, and *engineering*. On the whole, I feel that it is *much better* to watch educational programs.

Guided Response 2 Entertainment Programs
02-26

Although some people enjoy watching educational programs, I prefer watching *entertainment programs*. To begin with, I want to *relax* when I watch television. I watch TV in order to *clear my head*. I don't want to have to worry about the world and its *problems*. Furthermore, watching entertainment shows can *improve* my mood. For example, when I watch comedies, I feel happier and *less stressed*. Considering this, I would rather watch entertainment programs than *educational ones*.

Related Topics
p.71

Sample Response

Answers may vary.

4

Agree	Disagree
• teaches people not to think for themselves	• many educational programs
• makes people fat and lazy	• news and sport programs are good for people

5

Alone	With My Friends
• can relax and just watch the program	• talk about what I am watching with them
• relieve stress while alone	• enjoy watching games with other people

---

● Chapter | 04 Integrated Speaking

Task 2 Adding Kitchens to Dormitories

Reading
p.72

Analyzing

1 Ⓑ

2 Ⓑ

3 Ⓒ

Listening
p.73

Script & Notes 02-27

M: I think the writer of this letter makes a good argument. We students should have kitchens in our dormitories.

W: Oh, yeah? I'm not sure that adding kitchens to the dorms would be very beneficial.

M: Huh? What do you mean?

W: Well, think about it. Where in the dorms can the university put kitchens?

M: Um, I suppose they could be installed in the breakrooms.

W: That's right. We need a place to unwind in our dorms after studying all day. If the school installs kitchens, then our break areas will be taken away.

M: Hmm. I hadn't considered that.

W: And college students are busy anyway. Every day, we have to go to classes, study, and participate in club activities. We don't really have any free time. To me, it seems unrealistic to think that college students have enough time to learn how to cook.

M: Maybe you're right. Maybe we don't need kitchens after all.

> *Notes*
>
> The woman **disagrees** with the letter.
>
> **Reason 1:** *kitchens have to be installed in breakrooms; students need places to unwind after studying*
>
> **Reason 2:** *college students are busy; every day go to classes, study, clubs; do not have enough free time to learn cooking*
>
> **Key Words and Details:** *students should have kitchens; install in breakrooms; students need places to unwind; students busy; unrealistic*

Summarizing

Main Idea

The woman does not believe that the university should *install kitchens* in the dorms.

Reason 1

Her first concern is that the kitchens would have to be installed in the *breakrooms*. This means that students would have no place to *unwind* after studying.

Reason 2

The woman's second concern is that students *are too busy* to learn how to cook. She claims that students do not have time because they have to *attend classes* and study.

Synthesizing

1 The writer's main argument is that the university needs to *install kitchens in the dorms*.

2 At first, the man supports the plan, but by the end of the conversation, he *does not support it*.

3 The woman argues against the letter's claim that students *have enough time* to learn how to cook.

Speaking
p.74

Guided Response
02-28

The man and the woman are talking about a letter

asking the university to *install kitchens* in the dorms. While the man supports the plan, the woman *does not*. Her first argument is that the *break areas* in the dorms will have to be *removed*. She feels that students need places to *unwind* after studying. Next, the woman claims that college students are *busy*. She believes that it is *unrealistic* to think that college students have enough time to *learn how to cook*.

● Chapter | 04 Integrated Speaking

Task 3 Psychology: Anchoring Bias

■ Reading   p.75

Analyzing

1 Ⓐ

2 Ⓑ

3 Ⓐ

■ Listening   p.76

Script & Notes 02-29

Professor: Anchoring bias affects us all at times. The results may be good sometimes. However, that's not always true. Let me give you a personal example.

Last week, I decided to purchase a new office chair. I went online and found a store that specializes in office chairs. I found the exact chair that I wanted. I noticed that the original price was $450. However, the store was selling the chair for only $300. I was really impressed with that sale price. I immediately ordered it and had it delivered to my home.

When the chair arrived, my wife took a look at it. Then, she checked out some websites. Do you know what happened? She found other places were selling that chair for even cheaper prices. In that situation, I suffered from anchoring bias. I trusted the first bit of information I learned about the chair. And that turned out to be a bad decision.

Notes

Topic: *anchoring bias can have results that are not always positive*

Detail 1: *purchased a new office chair; original price was $450; was selling for $300*
was impressed with the price; ordered the chair

Detail 2: *wife checked out some websites; found places selling cheaper chairs*

---

suffered from anchoring bias; trusted the first information he learned

Key Words: *new office chair; original price; impressed; cheaper prices; anchoring bias; trusted*

Summarizing

Topic

The professor talks about a *personal experience*. He says that it shows how *anchoring bias* does not always have good results.

Detail 1

First, the professor says that he found an office chair online. Its *original price* was $450, but it was selling for $300. He ordered the chair and had it *delivered*.

Detail 2

The professor says that *his wife* checked some other websites. She found the chair *available* for cheaper prices. The professor had trusted the first piece of information he learned.

Synthesizing

1 Anchoring bias is when a person trusts the first piece of information learned about *a topic*.

2 He saw the original price was *$450*, but the chair was selling for only *$300*.

3 He *trusted* the first price that he saw and did not check other websites.

■ Speaking   p.77

Guided Response   02-30

The professor talks about buying an *office chair*. He says he found a chair online. It was selling for a *good price*, so he bought it. Later, the *professor's wife* searched some other *websites*. She found the chair available for even *lower prices*. In this case, the professor trusted the first information he learned about the chair. That was an example of *anchoring bias*. In anchoring bias, a person *compares* the first information learned to other information. In this case, the professor had a *bad result*.

Task 4 Human Biology: Different Types of Tears

■ Listening   p.78

`Script & Notes` 02-31

Professor: Over the course of a lifetime, most people produce millions of tears. You might think that all tears are the same, but there are actually several types of tears. Really. It's true! Let me explain in detail to give you a better idea.

I'm sure you all know that each time you blink, you produce tears. These are called blinking tears. They serve a couple purposes. One purpose is keeping the eyes moist and removing dust. This isn't all though. Blinking tears also contain substances that fight against bacterial infections. In fact, blinking tears are actually part of the immune system. So the tears we make when we blink work to keep our eyes healthy.

Then there are crying tears. Whenever we feel strong emotions—emotional stress, suffering, physical pain, and even joy—we produce crying tears. So it's no surprise that crying tears are produced by the part of our bodies that controls our emotions. These tears contain proteins and natural painkillers. As a result, we actually make ourselves feel better when we produce crying tears.

`Notes`

Topic: *different types of tears*

Detail 1: *blinking tears; keep eye moist and remove dust*
fight against bacterial infections

Detail 2: *crying tears; produced when we feel strong emotions*
contain proteins and natural painkillers

Key Words: *several types of tears; keep eyes moist; immune system; strong emotion; natural painkillers*

Summarizing

Topic

In the listening passage, the professor talks about *two different types* of tears.

Detail 1

The first type of tears is *blinking tears*. These keep the eyes *moist* and remove dust. They also fight against *bacterial infections*.

Detail 2

The other type of tears is *crying tears*. These are produced when we feel *strong emotions*. These contain proteins and act as *natural painkillers*.

■ Speaking   p.79

Guided Response   02-32

The professor's lecture focuses on two different types of *tears*. The first type of tears she discusses is *blinking tears*. These tears are *produced* when we blink. They keep the *eyes moist* and remove dust. Blinking tears are also part of our *immune system* as they help fight against *bacterial infections*. The professor then talks about *crying tears*. These are produced whenever we feel *strong emotions*. Crying tears contain proteins and *natural painkillers*. Producing crying tears helps us *feel better*.

● Chapter | 05 Independent Writing

Task 1 Spending Vacations at Home vs. Traveling

■ Brainstorming   p.82

Choice 1 Staying at Home

Reason 1: is more relaxing

Details: read books and play video games; spend all day lying in bed

Reason 2: can also save money

Details: plane tickets and hotels are expensive; do not have to pay for attractions

Choice 2 Traveling

Reason 1: can escape from my regular life

Details: meet many new people; experience new places

Reason 2: is also a lot of fun

Details: visit amusement parks; swim in the ocean

■ Organizing
Answers may vary.

My Choice: *Staying at Home*

First Reason: *able to relax*

Details: *read books, play video games, or do
                nothing at all*

Second Reason: *also saves money*

Details: *vacations can cost thousands of dollars*

My Choice: *Traveling*

First Reason: *can escape from my regular life*

Details: *experience new and exciting places*

Second Reason: *is also a lot of fun*

Details: *visit amusement parks or swim in the ocean*

■ Speaking
p.84

Guided Response 1 Staying at Home
02-33

During my time off from school, I enjoy staying *at home*.
I feel this way for two reasons. The first is that staying at
home is *relaxing*. I can read books, play *video games*, or
do nothing at all. I also prefer staying home because it
saves money. Vacations can *cost* thousands of dollars.
To me, this is a *waste* of money. On the whole, I would
much rather *stay home* during vacation.

Guided Response 2 Traveling
02-34

I like to *travel* whenever I have time off. For one,
traveling gives me the chance to *escape* from my
regular life. I can experience new and *exciting places*.
Another reason I like traveling is that it is *a lot of fun*. I
can visit an amusement park or swim in *the ocean*. This
is more *exciting* than staying at home. Some people
may enjoy staying home when they have time off. As for
me, *traveling* is much better.

■ Related Topics
p.85

Sample Response

Answers may vary.

4

Agree	Disagree
• *lots of time to learn a new skill* • *many classes available to take*	• *would rather relax* • *work part time so can't do other activities*

5

Agree	Disagree
• *can see more places* • *can travel farther away from home*	• *don't like being away for too long* • *get tired if take long trips*

● Chapter │ 05 Integrated Speaking

Task 2 School Newspaper No Longer to Be
Printed

■ Reading
p.86

Analyzing

1 Ⓑ

2 Ⓐ

3 Ⓑ

■ Listening
p.87

`Script & Notes` 02-35

M: Did you see this announcement? The school is
going to cease printing the newspaper. Tomorrow's
edition will be the last one ever.

W: Is that so? I know you read the school newspaper
every day. How do you feel about this decision?

M: That's a good question. Hmm . . . I guess I kind
of have mixed feelings. I mean, uh, I support this
decision by the school. After all, the school has
budget problems. And papers cost a lot to print.

W: That's true.

M: So it's a good idea to go entirely online. That's
especially true if few students are reading the paper.

W: But you said you have mixed feelings. What don't
you like about this decision?

M: I actually enjoy picking up a physical newspaper
and reading it. I often do that during lunch. Reading
a paper online is okay. But to me, reading an actual
paper is a much better experience.

> *Notes*
>
> The man **has mixed feelings about** the university's
> plan.
>
> **Reason:** *school has budget problems; papers are
>   expensive to print; good idea to go online;
>   likes reading a physical newspaper; better
>   experience than reading a paper online*

Key Words and Details: *have mixed feelings;*
support this decision; budget problems;
cost a lot to print; enjoy picking up a
physical newspaper; reading a paper online
is okay; much better experience

Summarizing

Main Idea

The man has mixed feelings. He understands why the university made the decision, but he is not completely *happy*.

Reason 1

The school has *budget problems*, and printing a newspaper is expensive. So it's a good idea to *go online* if *few students* are reading the paper.

Reason 2

He likes *picking up* a physical newspaper and reading it. Doing that is a better *experience* for him than reading online.

Synthesizing

1   The school will stop *printing* the school newspaper.

2   The man says that he has *mixed feelings* about the announcement.

3   He says that he often reads a *physical newspaper* during lunch.

■ Speaking   p.88

Guided Response   02-36

The speakers talk about the school's decision to *stop printing* the school newspaper. The man has mixed feelings about this decision. First, he understands the decision because printing a paper is *expensive*. He mentions that the school has *budget problems*. So he thinks it is smart to stop printing the paper since *few students* are reading it. However, he comments that he also dislikes the decision. For him, reading a *physical newspaper* is better than reading the *online version* of the paper.

Task 3 Animal Science: Echolocation

■ Reading   p.89

Analyzing

1   Ⓒ

2   Ⓐ

3   Ⓐ

■ Listening   p.90

Script & Notes   02-37

Professor: There are several animals that rely on echolocation to survive. But today, I want to focus on an animal of the night—an animal that scares many people. Of course, I'm talking about bats.

Most bats live in caves and other dark places. To get around these places, bats must use echolocation. Here's how they do it. When bats fly, they make high-pitched sounds. These sounds shoot out like lasers and bounce back to the bats. Bats figure out where the sounds are coming from and how long it takes for them to come back. Based on this, bats create images of their environment in their minds. And do you know what else? Bats even use echolocation for hunting. They are so sensitive that they can find the smallest insects in caves. That's how bats fly and hunt without sight. Amazing, isn't it?

Notes

Topic: *bats use echolocation*

Detail 1: *live in dark places; make high-pitched*
        sounds
        sounds shoot out like lasers

Detail 2: *figure out where sounds come from and*
        how long they take to come back; create
        images of their environment sensitive enough
        to find the smallest insects

Key Words: *high-pitched sounds; sounds bounce*
        back; create images of environment;
        use for hunting; find the smallest insects

Summarizing

Topic

The instructor mainly talks about how bats *use echolocation*.

Detail 1

She begins by describing the *high-pitched* sounds bats make. She explains that they shoot out like *lasers* and bounce back to the bats.

Detail 2

The bats figure out *where* the sounds are coming from and *how long* it takes for them to come back. This way, the bats can create an *image* of their environment. They can also *hunt* in this way.

Synthesizing

1. They use echolocation to understand the shape of an area and to *hunt for food*.

2. The sounds created by bats shoot out like lasers and *bounce back to the bats*.

3. Bats use echolocation to hunt *small insects*.

■ Speaking   p.91

Guided Response   02-38

The reading passage and the lecture both deal with the topic of *echolocation*. The passage gives some background *information* about the topic. The instructor explains this topic by talking about *bats*. According to the instructor, bats make *high-pitched* sounds when they fly. These sounds shoot out like lasers and *bounce back* to the bats. The bats can use these sounds to create an image of their *environment*. She also mentions that bats hunt *small insects* by using echolocation.

● Chapter | 05 Integrated Speaking

Task 4 Business: Ineffective Logos

■ Listening   p.92

Script & Notes   02-39

Professor: Our world is filled with logos. When you see a red and white cola can, you know it's a Coca-Cola. This is an effective logo because it grabs our attention and makes us want to buy the product. But not all logos are effective. Let me explain why.

As we all know, different colors create different emotions in us. And that's why choosing the right color for a logo is so important. But one healthcare company apparently didn't know this. You see, its logo was black, the color of death. Would you buy healthcare from a company with a black logo?

I wouldn't. And neither did anybody else. Before long, this company went out of business simply because its logo was the wrong color.

The appearance of a logo also matters a lot. The appearance of a company's logo should match its products. Otherwise, problems can happen. This was the case for a small computer company. It had great products, but its logo looked old fashioned. People who saw the logo thought the company's products were outdated, too. Obviously, this was bad for business. So the company quickly made a more modern logo. What was the result? The business became much more successful almost immediately.

Notes

Topic: *effective logos grab our attention and make us want to buy the product; but not all logos are effective*

Detail 1: *different colors create different emotions; choosing the right color is important healthcare company had a black logo; went out of business*

Detail 2: *appearance of logo also important; should match products computer company had old-fashioned logo; customers thought their products were outdated*

Key Words: *grabs attention; not all logos effective; healthcare company; black; color of death; went out of business; old-fashioned logo; outdated*

Summarizing

Topic

The professor discusses *ineffective* product logos in his lecture.

Detail 1

The *color* of a logo is a very important. One healthcare company had a *black logo*. Black is the color of *death*. So the company went *out of business*.

Detail 2

The *appearance* of a logo also matters. The logo should *match* the company's products. A small computer company had an *old-fashioned* logo. So people thought its *products* were outdated. It made a *more modern logo*, and the business became successful.

The professor talks about *ineffective* product logos in his lecture. He first mentions the importance of *color*. He describes a *healthcare company* that had a black logo. Black is the color of *death*. As a result, the company *went out of business*. Next, the professor talks about logo *appearance*. He describes a computer company with an *old-fashioned* logo. People saw the logo and thought the company's products were *outdated*. So it made a *more modern* logo. Afterward, it became *successful*.

● Chapter | 06 Independent Writing

Task 1 Store-Bought Presents vs. Homemade Presents

■ **Brainstorming** p.96

Choice 1 Store-Bought Presents

Reason 1: come in a wider variety

Details: cellphones and other electronics; designer clothing

Reason 2: also more practical

Details: use new television for years; homemade gifts used a few times

Choice 2 Homemade Presents

Reason 1: have special meanings

Details: takes time to make gift; care about me very much

Reason 2: also made especially for me

Details: sister made chocolates; cannot buy in store

■ **Organizing**

Answers may vary.

My Choice: *Store-Bought Presents*

First Reason: *come in a wider variety*

Details: *cellphones and other electronics to a brand-new car*

Second Reason: *also more practical*

Details: *use new high-definition television for years while homemade gifts can be used only a few times*

My Choice: *Homemade Presents*

First Reason: *have special meanings*

Details: *takes time to make gift, which means that the person cares about me very much*

Second Reason: *also made especially for me*

Details: *sister made chocolates; not able to buy in store*

■ **Speaking** p.98

Guided Response 1 Store-Bought Presents 02-41

I enjoy receiving homemade presents. Nevertheless, I prefer *store-bought presents*. I feel this way for two reasons. For starters, store-bought gifts come in a *wider variety* than homemade gifts. To be specific, I can receive anything from a *cellphone* to a brand-new car. My second reason is that store-bought gifts tend to be more *practical*. For example, I can receive a high-definition television that I can use *every day* for years. However, most homemade gifts can only be used *a few times*.

Guided Response 2 Homemade Presents 02-42

Most people prefer store-bought presents. However, I would rather receive *homemade presents*. First of all, homemade presents have *special meanings*. I know the person spent a lot of time making the gift, so that means that the person *cares* about me very much. Another reason I prefer homemade presents is that they are made *especially* for me. To give an example, my sister made *some mango-flavored chocolates* for me. I cannot *buy* these in a store, so her gift was very special to me.

■ **Related Topics** p.99

Sample Response

Answers may vary.

4

Agree	Disagree
• *don't want some students to be left out*	• *don't invite people you don't like*
• *good way to make friends with classmates*	• *may not have enough room for everyone if the class is big*

5

One Big Present	Many Smaller Presents
• can get something useful	• smaller presents = more meaningful
• would rather unwrap one present than many	• lots of fun to get many presents

● Chapter | **06 Integrated Speaking**

Task 2 Moving Student Orientation

■ Reading

p.100

Analyzing

1 Ⓒ

2 Ⓐ

3 Ⓐ

■ Listening

p.101

`Script & Notes` 02-43

M: So this student wants to move the orientation program to the summer? Personally, I think having it during the fall is fine.

W: Really? Why do you think so?

M: It's just that during the summer, the campus is practically deserted. Most of the students are on break. Plus, many facilities are shut down.

W: That's true. The school basically becomes a ghost town.

M: Pretty much. So if the new students visit during summer, then they won't be able to see what the campus is really like.

W: Yeah, that's a good point.

M: Besides, most people go on vacation during the summer, don't they?

W: I would say so. I know I'm away on vacation every summer.

M: Right. So most students probably can't come to orientation during the summer anyway. And what's the point of having an orientation if no one can participate?

`Notes`

The man **disagrees** with the letter.

Reason 1: *campus is practically deserted; most students are on break; facilities shut down; cannot see what campus is really like*

Reason 2: *most people go on vacation during summer; students cannot come to orientation; no point in having orientation*

Key Words and Details: *having the orientation during fall is fine; campus deserted; facilities are shut down; cannot come to orientation during summer*

Summarizing

Main Idea

The man feels that having the orientation during the fall is *fine*. In this way, he *disagrees* with the letter.

Reason 1

For his first argument, the man states that the campus is *deserted* during the summer. Because of this, the students cannot see what the campus is *really like*.

Reason 2

The man also notes that most people *go on vacation* during the summer. This means they cannot *come* to orientation during the summer, making the orientation *pointless*.

Synthesizing

1 It would benefit new students by giving them more time to *transition* into college life.

2 The woman says that the campus is practically a *ghost town*.

3 He feels that most students *cannot attend* because they will be on vacation.

■ Speaking

p.102

Guided Response 02-44

The man feels that the orientation should remain in the *fall*. His first argument is that the campus is mostly *deserted* during the summer. The man claims that most students are *on break* and that many *facilities* are closed. As a result, the students will not see what the campus is *really like*. The man then points out that most people go *on vacation* during the summer. This means that most students will not be able to *participate* in a summer orientation program.

Task 3 Sociology: Sibling Rivalry

■ Reading
p.103

Analyzing

1 Ⓐ

2 Ⓐ

3 Ⓒ

■ Listening
p.104

`Script & Notes` 02-45

Professor: Let me tell you about the sibling rivalry between my own children and how I dealt with it.

I had two boys. They were born three years apart. Because of this, my sons fought with each other all the time. All this fighting caused my family a lot of stress. After a while, I wanted to bring peace back to my household. So here's what I did. One thing I always made sure to do was recognize each of my son's unique talents and abilities. One of my boys was an excellent athlete. The other was a good singer. I made sure to praise them both. This made them both feel special. I also gave them a chance to work out their differences themselves. You might be surprised that even young children are willing to make compromises and sacrifices if you give them the chance to do so.

> **Notes**
>
> **Topic:** *dealing with sibling rivalry*
>
> **Detail 1:** *recognize each son's unique abilities; one son was an athlete; other was singer; praised both children; made them feel special*
>
> **Detail 2:** *let children work out differences themselves; even young children able to make compromises*
>
> **Key Words:** *boys fought all the time; caused family a lot of stress; praise both; make compromises, sacrifices*

Summarizing

Topic

The professor talks about methods to *reduce* sibling rivalry.

Detail 1

The first method the professor used was *recognizing*

each son's abilities. She praised both boys for their *unique talents*. This made them both *feel special*.

Detail 2

The professor also let her children *work out* their differences themselves. She explains that even young children are able to make *compromises*.

Synthesizing

1 They often develop feelings of *jealousy* toward each other.

2 The sibling rivalry between the professor's sons caused her family *a lot of stress*.

3 Praising the sons for their talents made them both *feel special*.

■ Speaking
p.105

Guided Response
02-46

The reading passage describes *sibling rivalry*. This is a type of *competition* between brothers and sisters. They often fight for the *attention* of their parents. In her lecture, the professor describes *two methods* she used to reduce sibling rivalry between her sons. The first method was recognizing the *unique talents* of her sons. She gave both boys praise. This made them both *feel special*. Her second method was to let her sons work out their *differences* themselves. The professor explains that even young children are able to make *compromises*.

● Chapter | 06 Integrated Speaking

Task 4 Animal Science: Earthworms Help Plant Growth

■ Listening
p.106

`Script & Notes` 02-47

Professor: For a long time, people thought of garden worms as pests. What they didn't realize is that worms actually help plants grow. The reason for this is simple: Worms help keep the soil healthy. Don't believe me? All right, then listen to this.

First of all, worms increase the amount of nutrients in the soil. You see, worms eat organic materials . . . They eat things such as leaves and grass. They digest these things and break them down into nutrients that plants can use. The worms leave their droppings as they crawl through the soil. The droppings then act as fertilizer for plants. In fact, worm droppings are better fertilizer than most manmade products.

Not only that, but worms also create topsoil. Just think about how worms live. They move through the soil and create tunnels. This moves the lower layers of the dirt to the top and vice versa. So what does this do? It increases the amount of air in the soil, which introduces more nutrients. And let's not forget the tunnels themselves. Worm tunnels allow water to pass through the soil more easily. This helps keep the soil moist.

Notes

Topic: *earthworms; help plants grow; help keep soil healthy*

Detail 1: *increase the amount of nutrients in the soil break down organic materials into nutrients plants can use; worm droppings excellent fertilizer*

Detail 2: *create topsoil move lower layers of dirt to top; increases air in soil and adds nutrients; tunnels allow water to pass through soil*

Key Words: *increase nutrients in soil; organic materials; move lower layers of dirt; increase air in soil; allow water to pass easily*

Summarizing

Topic

In the lecture, the instructor explains how earthworms help *plants* grow. He says they do this by keeping the soil *healthy*.

Detail 1

The first way they do this is by increasing the amount of *nutrients* in the soil. They eat leaves and grass and break them down into *materials* plants can use. This happens because worms leave their *droppings* in the soil.

Detail 2

Worms also create *topsoil*. As they crawl through the dirt, worms move the *lower layers* of soil to the top. This introduces more *nutrients* into the soil. Their tunnels also allow more *water* to pass through the soil easily.

Speaking   p.107

Guided Response   02-48

The instructor explains how earthworms help *plants*

---

grow by keeping the soil healthy. For one, earthworms increase the amount of *nutrients* in the soil. They eat *organic materials* such as leaves and grass. Later, their droppings act as an *excellent fertilizer*. The instructor then talks about how worms create *topsoil*. He says that worms move the *lower layers* of soil to the top as they crawl through the soil. This introduces more *air* and nutrients into the soil. Their *tunnels* also help water pass through the soil.

● Chapter | 07 Independent Writing

Task 1 Students Should Have Part-Time Job Experience

■ Brainstorming   p.110

Choice 1 **Have Part-Time Job Experience**

Reason 1: teaches time-management skills

Details: balance working and studying; learn to study efficiently

Reason 2: also learn value of money

Details: live without wasting money; students usually do not have much money

---

Choice 2 **Focus on Studying**

Reason 1: should focus on getting good grades

Details: working students have lower grades; cannot get scholarships with poor grades

Reason 2: also do not pay high salaries

Details: little economic benefit; cannot save much money

■ Organizing

Answers may vary.

> **My Choice:** *Have Part-Time Job Experience*
>
> **First Reason:** *teaches students time-management skills*
>
> **Details:** *must learn to balance work and study time*
>
> **Second Reason:** *also teaches students value of money*
>
> **Details:** *live without wasting money; students usually do not have a lot of money*

My Choice: *Focus on Studying*

First Reason: *should focus only on studying*

Details: *main responsibility getting good grades; students with jobs have lower grades*

Second Reason: *most part-time jobs do not pay high salaries*

Details: *little economic benefit to work these jobs*

Speaking

p.112

___
Guided Response 1   Have Part-Time Job Experience   02-49

I am convinced that students should have *part-time job experience* before going to college. First of all, I believe that having a job teaches students *time-management skills*. Students with jobs learn how to *balance* their work time and study time. I also believe that work experience helps students because it teaches them the *value of money*. Working students learn how to live without *wasting* money. This is important because most college students do not have *a lot of* money.

___
Guided Response 2   Focus on Studying   02-50

I disagree that students should have *work experience* before entering college. Instead, I believe that students should focus *only on studying*. First, the main responsibility of students is getting *good grades*. However, students who have part-time jobs usually have *lower grades* than students who do not work. On top of this, most part-time jobs do not pay *high salaries*. So there is little *economic benefit* for students to work at these jobs. Overall, I strongly believe that students should *concentrate* only on studying.

Related Topics

p.113

___
Sample Response

Answers may vary.

4

Agree	Disagree
• no need for students to work many hours	• some students need to support their families
• studying is more important than working	• if students can keep their grades up, let them work as much as they want

5

Agree	Disagree
• employers take advantage of cheap labor	• students have no experience so get paid little
• students have no choice but to take low-paying jobs	• part-time jobs always pay poorly

● Chapter | 07 Integrated Speaking

Task 2 Fitness Center Renovation

Reading

p.114

___
Analyzing

1 Ⓑ

2 Ⓒ

3 Ⓑ

Listening

p.115

Script & Notes   02-51

M: Take a look at this. The fitness center is going to be closed for the entire semester. Now where can I work out?

W: Yeah, it's too bad that we can't exercise there this semester. Even so, renovating the fitness center is probably for the best.

M: What do you mean?

W: Well, take the exercise machines. Most of them are really old. A lot of times, they are broken. So it's hard to get a good workout.

M: You have a point there.

W: And the facilities are too small now. The university has many more students now than it used to. So the fitness center is always crowded.

M: Yeah . . . You're right about that. I always have to wait to use any of the fitness machines.

W: But once the school enlarges the fitness center, that won't be a problem anymore.

M: Maybe I should actually be happy about the school's plan, huh?

Notes

The woman **agrees** with the announcement.

Reason 1: *exercise machines are really old; usually broken; hard to get a good workout*

Reason 2: *facilities are too small; university has many more students than before; fitness center is always really crowded*

Key Words and Details: *renovating for the best; machines really old; usually broken; hard to get a good workout; facilities too small; center always crowded*

Task 3 Business: Giving Samples

Reading   p.117

Analyzing

1   (B)

2   (A)

3   (B)

Summarizing

Main Idea

The woman believes the renovations are *for the best*.

Reason 1

First, the woman explains that most of the exercise machines are *really old*. A lot of times, they are *broken*. This makes it hard to get a *good workout*.

Reason 2

Next, the woman argues that the facilities are *too small*. She notes that the university has many *more students* than it used to. As a result, the fitness center is always *crowded*.

Synthesizing

1   The renovations will make the exercise areas and the *locker rooms* larger.

2   She states that the university has *many more students* than it used to.

3   He says that he usually has to wait to use *any exercise equipment*.

Speaking   p.116

Guided Response   02-52

The speakers are discussing their university's plan to *renovate* the fitness center. The woman feels the plan is *for the best*. She gives two reasons to *support* her opinion. The first is that the *exercise machines* are very old. She claims that the machines are usually *broken*. This makes it hard to get a *good workout*. Furthermore, the woman says that the facilities are *too small*. The university has *many more students* than it used to, so the fitness center is always *crowded*.

Listening   p.118

Script & Notes   02-53

Professor: Okay, let's talk more about giving away samples. To help you understand the benefits of giving samples, I'll explain to you how one small business became successful by giving samples to its customers.

All right, so this shop sold DVDs. For a long time, it struggled to make a profit. Why? Basically, most of the shop's customers browsed the movies, but few of them bought any. The owner realized this and came up with a plan. He decided to let customers watch the first 10 minutes of any DVD they wanted. This was long enough to let the customers know whether or not they were interested in the movie. It also made them want to see more. And do you know what? The plan worked wonderfully. After the owner let customers sample DVDs, more and more people started buying them. As a result, the store's profits went way up.

Notes

Topic: *giving samples to attract more customers*

Detail 1: *DVD shop struggled to make profit; customers browsed movies; few customers bought movies*

Detail 2: *owner let customers watch movies for 10 minutes; customers could decide if interested; profits went way up*

Key Words: *benefits of giving samples; small business became successful; browsed movies; watch first 10 minutes; profits up*

Summarizing

Topic

The lecturer explains how businesses can attract more customers by *giving free samples*.

Detail 1

He first talks about a DVD shop that *struggled* to make a profit. Customers would *browse* movies but not buy them.

Detail 2

The owner of the store decided to let customers watch the first *10 minutes* of movies. This let customers decide if they were *interested* in the movies. As a result, the shop's *profits* increased.

Synthesizing

1   It is difficult for businesses to sell more products because customers *do not want to try new products*.

2   The problem the business had is that most of its shoppers did not *buy any DVDs*.

3   The example proves the argument because it shows how giving samples let a business *sell more products*.

■ Speaking

p.119

Guided Response

02-54

The passage explains how businesses can sell more products by giving *free samples*. The lecturer *explains* this idea by giving an example. She talks about a *DVD shop* that had trouble selling its products. Most of its customers would *browse*, but few of them would *buy anything*. So the owner decided to let shoppers watch the *first 10 minutes* of DVDs. This allowed them to *decide* which DVDs they wanted to buy. The owner's plan worked and allowed the store to generate more *profits*.

● Chapter | 07 Integrated Speaking

Task 4 Agriculture: Organic Farming

■ Listening

p.122

`Script & Notes` 02-55

Professor: Let me talk about organic farming for a moment. It's becoming popular nowadays. And I'd like to tell you why.

There are several advantages to organic farming. Now, uh, one feature of it is that farmers don't use any pesticides or weedkillers. Instead, they rely upon natural means to kill insects and to get rid of weeds. How does this benefit people? It's simple. Those chemicals often get on crops which are harvested. Later, people may consume the chemicals when they eat the fruits or vegetables. But organically grown crops have no chemicals on them. So people won't get sick or be harmed by them. As a result, people can stay healthy by eating organic crops.

In addition, organic farming doesn't rely upon any chemical fertilizers. Farmers use other natural methods to replace nutrients in the soil. For instance, they might put cow or chicken manure on the soil. They might use crop rotation as well. And many farmers plant crops which are good for the soil. You know, these plants put nutrients into the soil rather than taking them out. These methods all help the environment. Farmers don't harm the earth because they don't put chemicals in the soil. In fact, they actively improve the environment.

> *Notes*
>
> **Topic:** *organic farming*
>
> **Detail 1:** *don't use pesticides or weedkillers; use natural means to kill insects and weeds no chemicals on crops when harvested people not sick or harmed by eating them*
>
> **Detail 2:** *no chemical fertilizers use manure; do crop rotation; plant crops good for the soil improve the environment tunnels allow water to pass through soil*
>
> **Key Words:** *pesticides; weedkiller; natural means; no chemicals; won't get sick or be harmed; chemical fertilizers; cow or chicken manure; crop rotation; put nutrients into the soil; improve the environment*

Summarizing

Topic

The topic of the lecture is *organic farming*.

Detail 1

Organic farmers do not use pesticides or weedkillers. Instead, they *kill* insects and weeds by using natural means. Their *crops* have no chemicals on them when they are *harvested*. So people are not *harmed* by eating the crops.

Detail 2

Organic farmers also do not use *chemical fertilizers*.

They use *manure* and crop rotation instead. Some farmers plant crops good for *the soil*. Those crops put *nutrients* into the soil. As a result, they help improve the *environment*.

▮ Speaking

p.123

Guided Response

02-56

The professor lectures on *organic farming*. He says it has some *advantages*. The first is that organic farmers use *natural means* to kill insects and weeds. As a result, there are no *harmful chemicals* on their crops when they are *harvested*. So people are not hurt by *eating* them. Second, the professor says that organic farmers don't use *chemical fertilizers*. Instead, they use manure and crop rotation. They also plant crops that *add* nutrients to the soil. In this way, organic farmers help *improve* the environment.

● Chapter │ 08 Independent Writing

Task 1 Driving Cars vs. Taking Public Transportation

▮ Brainstorming

p.124

Choice 1 Driving Cars

Advantage 1: go anywhere anytime

Advantage 2: no waiting or crowds

Detail: don't wait at airport or take crowded buses and trains

Disadvantage 1: tiring to drive a lot

Disadvantage 2: easy to get lost

Detail: happened to father one time

Choice 2 Taking Public Transportation

Advantage 1: convenient to take

Advantage 2: cheaper than renting a car

Detail: get to destinations quickly

Disadvantage 1: hard to understand bus and subway schedules

Disadvantage 2: not available everywhere

Detail: have to walk to some places

▮ Organizing

Answers may vary.

> **My Choice:** *Driving Cars*
>
> **Advantages:** *go anywhere you want to; no long waits*
>
> **Details:** *no long lines at airports; no crowds on buses or trains*
>
> **Disadvantages:** *get tired driving; get lost*
>
> **Details:** *father got lost on a trip once*

> **My Choice:** *Taking Public Transportation*
>
> **Advantages:** *convenient; cheaper than renting a vehicle*
>
> **Details:** *can get to destinations very fast*
>
> **Disadvantages:** *hard to understand schedules; not always available*
>
> **Details:** *might have to walk to places*

▮ Speaking

p.126

Guided Response 1 Driving Cars

02-57

There are many advantages to *driving cars* when people travel. One is that they can *go anywhere* they want at any time. In addition, travelers who drive do not have to wait *a long time* for flights at airports. They don't have to take crowded *buses or trains* either. However, there are also some *disadvantages* to driving cars. It can be *tiring* to drive from place to place while traveling. Travelers can also easily *get lost* driving in new cities. This happened to my father once.

Guided Response 2 Taking Public Transportation

02-58

I can think of a few *advantages* of taking public transportation on a trip. First, public transportation is *very convenient*. It can get people from *place to place* quickly. It is also much *cheaper* than renting a car while on a trip. On the other hand, there are some disadvantages. If a traveler is in a *foreign country*, it can be difficult to understand the bus or subway *schedule*. And public transportation is not *available* everywhere. So travelers may need to walk at times.

Related Topics

Sample Response

Answers may vary.

4

Advantages	Disadvantages
• have plenty of time to travel • can visit multiple places	• can make you tired • easy to go over budget

5

Advantages	Disadvantages
• get some rest • stay in a comfortable environment	• can be boring • stressful to stay at place all the time

● Chapter | 08 Integrated Speaking

Task 2 Spring Concert Series

Reading

p.128

Analyzing

1 Ⓑ

2 Ⓐ

3 Ⓒ

Listening

p.129

Script & Notes 02-59

M: These concerts should be a lot of fun. I'm really looking forward to going to them.

W: Yeah, maybe. Still, I think there are some drawbacks the student council didn't consider.

M: Such as?

W: Well, first of all, the students are busy. It's great to have entertainment on campus. But students just don't have enough time to go to concerts. We have a lot of homework and studying to do. And we need time to rest in the evenings, too.

M: I suppose. But it's not like students will be forced to go.

W: Yeah, but the performances will be held in the middle of campus, won't they?

M: Yes, on the lawn behind the student center.

W: Okay. You know, that's a main walking area. If many students go to the concerts, then it will be hard to get past that area. Plus, all those people standing on the lawn will kill the grass.

> *Notes*
>
> The woman **disagrees** with the announcement.
>
> **Reason 1:** *students are busy; do not have enough time to go to concerts; have to do homework, study, and rest*
>
> **Reason 2:** *concerts will be held in main walking area; hard to get past; students will kill the grass*
>
> **Key Words and Details:** *students are busy; homework, studying, resting; main walking area; hard to get past; kill the grass*

Summarizing

Main Idea

The woman believes the spring concert series has some important *drawbacks*.

Reason 1

For one, the woman worries that students are *too busy* to attend concerts. She says that students have to *study* and rest in the evenings.

Reason 2

The woman then notes that the performances will be held in a *main walking area*. If many students attend the concerts, it will be hard to *get past* the area. The students will also *kill the grass* on the lawn.

Synthesizing

1   The announcement states that the concerts will be held *on the back lawn of the student center*.

2   He says that students will not be *forced* to attend the concerts.

3   She says that the concerts will be held in the middle of campus in a main *walking area*.

Speaking

p.130

Guided Response

02-60

The speakers are talking about a *spring concert series* at their university. The woman feels there are some *important drawbacks* to having concerts on campus. First, the woman argues that students are *too busy* to attend concerts. They have to study and *rest* in the evenings. Furthermore, the woman notes that the concerts will be held in a main *walking area*. She worries that it will be hard to *get past* the area and that the students will *kill the grass* on the lawn.

● Chapter | 08 Integrated Speaking

Task 3 Psychology: Mental Accounting

Reading
p.131

Analyzing

1 Ⓒ

2 Ⓑ

3 Ⓑ

Listening
p.132

Script & Notes 02-61

Professor: Today, I'll share a personal experience to explain mental accounting to you.

All right, so when I was younger, I worked in an office. I used my income to pay my rent and bills. I saved the leftover money to buy a house. Sounds pretty logical, right? Well, I also had a second job. I worked as a waiter on the weekends.

This job earned me a nice extra income. The problem was that I created a different mental category for this income. You see, I decided in my head that all of the money from my waiter job would be used only for having fun. I didn't even consider adding this money to my savings. Because of my mental accounting, I ended up wasting all the money from the waiter job. If I had categorized the money differently, then I could have saved up for my house more quickly.

Notes

Topic: *the concept of mental accounting*

Detail 1: *instructor worked at an office; used income to pay rent and bills; saved leftover money toward buying house*

Detail 2: *worked as a waiter on weekends; created different mental category for income; used income only for fun; wasted all money*

Key Words: *worked at an office; paid rent and bills; second job; extra income; used only for fun*

Summarizing

Topic

In the listening, the instructor explains the concept of *mental accounting*.

Detail 1

First, the instructor talks about his experience as an *office worker*. He says that he used the income from this job to pay his *rent and bills*. He saved the *leftover* money so that he could buy a house.

Detail 2

Next, he says that he had a *second job* as a waiter. He explains that he used all of the money for *having fun*. He did this because he created a different *mental category* for his waiter income.

Synthesizing

1 It mentions that people do not *transfer* money from one category to another.

2 He explains that he did not consider using the money from his waiter job to *save for his house*.

3 He used all of that income only for *having fun*.

Speaking
p.133

Guided Response
02-62

The instructor describes *mental accounting* with a personal example. He begins by saying that he was an *office worker*. He used this income to pay his *rent and bills*. He used the *leftover money* to save for a house. The instructor also had a second job as a *waiter*. The income from this job was used only for *having fun*. He did not *consider* using this money to save for his house. This illustrates the concept in mental accounting that people do not *transfer* money across different categories.

● Chapter | 08 Integrated Speaking

Task 4 Animal Science: Electric Fish

Listening
p.134

Script & Notes 02-63

Professor: The oceans of the world are filled with unusual fish. But perhaps the most unusual among them are electric fish. These strange fish use their electricity in a couple of different ways.

First, I will talk about the best-known electric fish: the electric eel. Most of its body is made up of electric organs. With these organs, the electric eel is capable of generating very powerful shocks. In fact, it can create more than 500 volts of electricity. That's powerful enough to kill a horse. It uses these deadly shocks to stun other fish or to defend its territory. Generally, however, the electric eel mostly uses weaker shocks for hunting.

Of course, not all electric fish use electricity for defense or hunting. Others use it for navigation. This is the case with the knife fish. The knife fish lives in muddy waters. It can't use its sight to find objects in its environment. Instead, it "sees" by using a special organ in its skin. How does this work? Well, every living creature gives off a small electrical charge. The knife fish uses its special organ to detect these electrical charges. By doing this, the fish can find objects that are near it even if they're buried in mud.

Notes

Topic: *how electric fish use electricity*

Detail 1: *electric eels; most of body made up of electric organs*
generate very powerful shocks; used to stun and defend territory;
use weaker shocks for hunting

Detail 2: *knife fish; lives in muddy waters; cannot use sight for navigation*
uses special organ in skin to find objects;
detect electrical charge of living creatures

Key Words: *electric organs; stun other fish; defend territory; navigation; small electrical charge; detect objects*

Summarizing

Topic

The professor explains how *electric fish* use electricity.

Detail 1

For her first example, the professor talks about *electric eels*. She explains that electric eels generate *powerful shocks* to stun other fish and to *defend* their territory. However, eels usually use weaker shocks in order to *hunt*.

Detail 2

Next, the professor describes the *knife fish*. She says that knife fish uses a *special organ* in its skin for navigation. This organ *detects* the electrical charges given off by *living creatures*. With it, the knife fish can find *objects* in its environment.

The professor's lecture explains how *electric fish* use electricity. She first talks about the *electric eel*. She explains that most of an eel's body is made up of *electric organs*. It uses these organs to *generate* powerful shocks to stun other fish and to *defend* its territory. However, it only uses *weaker shocks* for hunting. Next, the professor talks about *knife fish*. This fish lives in *muddy waters*. So it cannot use sight for *navigation*. Instead, it uses a special organ in its skin to detect *electrical charges* given off by living creatures.

Part C

Task 1

Sample Response 1 **Agree**

I strongly agree with the statement. I think that elementary school children should not play computer games. First, computer games are a waste of time. I see many young children playing games for hours each day. Instead, they should be outside playing with their friends or reading books. In addition, computer games are not realistic. Young children often have difficulty separating fantasy from reality. Many computer games are violent. So elementary school children may come to believe that hurting or killing people is okay because they do that in computer games.

Sample Response 2 **Disagree**

Although some people want to ban elementary school children from playing computers games, I am not one of them. I believe computer games have some advantages for young children. First, many games teach children hand-eye coordination. For example, in shooting games, children have to aim properly to shoot objects on the screen. This can improve their physical skills. Other games require problem-solving skills. So elementary school children have to think about problems and figure out how to solve them. As a result, children can often benefit from playing computer games.

Task 2

Listening   03-03

W: Hey, Will, didn't you take that poetry class last semester?

M: I sure did. I'm really disappointed that the university has decided to get rid of the class.

W: But the university said that not enough students have been taking the class.

M: Personally, I think poetry classes should have only a few students. My class had five students, so the professor could personalize what we studied. It was easier for the professor to give us feedback, too.

W: That sounds nice.

M: But now students have to go all the way to State University to study poetry. That's just so inconvenient. I mean, it takes an hour to get there by bus. And most students don't have cars.

W: Yeah, going all the way there just to take one class would be a waste of time.

M: That's what I think. The school's plan is unfair and doesn't make a lot of sense.

Sample Response

The man and the woman are talking about their university's decision to remove a poetry class from the schedule. The university decided that not enough students were taking the class. The man disagrees with the decision for two reasons. His first reason is that poetry classes should have fewer students than other classes. This allows the professor to personalize what each student studies. Professors can also give feedback more easily. His second argument is that taking the class at another university is inconvenient. The other university is an hour away, and most students do not have cars.

Task 3

Listening   03-04

Professor: I'd like to finish my lecture by talking about the optimal foraging theory. Why don't we examine how crows forage for their meals?

A favorite meal of crows is shellfish. According to the optimal foraging theory, animals search for foods that are the highest in calories. So crows find the largest shellfish possible. This lets them consume a lot of calories at once without wasting energy on finding several shellfish to eat. However, opening shellfish can be difficult. Again, the optimal foraging theory predicts the crow's behavior. Crows carry the shellfish into the air and drop them onto a hard surface. Crows must choose the correct height for breaking the shell. If they fly too low, the shell won't break. This wastes energy. On the other hand, flying too high also wastes energy. So the crows fly at just the right height to break the shellfish.

Sample Response

In his lecture, the professor talks about the optimal foraging theory. To explain this, the professor discusses crows. He begins by stating that crows like to eat shellfish because they have many calories. As explained by the optimal foraging theory, crows eat the largest shellfish they can find. The reason is that they can consume a lot of calories without wasting too much energy. Then, the professor explains how crows break open shellfish. The crows fly just high enough to break the shellfish without wasting energy. This action is also explained by the optimal foraging theory.

Task 4

Listening

03-05

Professor: The Roman Empire was one of the largest empires in history. Just how were the Romans able to expand their territory so much? It's difficult to choose a single factor. But Roman technological developments played a major part.

The Romans possessed much more advanced technology than any other civilization at the time. One of them was concrete. Ancient Roman concrete was similar in strength to modern concrete. Can you believe it? The Romans used concrete to build all sorts of new structures, such as arches. With concrete, they were also able to construct durable bridges. These bridges allowed the Romans to move thousands of soldiers and civilians across lakes and rivers. This made it easy for the Romans to expand their territory across a large area.

But the bridges were only the first step. The Romans needed a way to bring water into their new cities. Their solution was to construct aqueducts. These manmade passages moved water from the mountains into the cities. Some aqueducts were more than 100 kilometers long. Amazing, isn't it? The aqueducts made it possible for the Romans to build great cities with high populations. In fact, most ancient Roman cities used as much water per person as today's cities.

Sample Response

The lecturer provides reasons why the Roman Empire could expand so much. The professor claims this happened because of technological developments. The first one she mentions was concrete. Ancient Roman concrete was very strong. It was used to build large bridges. These concrete bridges made it possible for thousands of Roman soldiers and civilians to cross lakes and rivers. As a result, the Romans were able to increase the size of their empire with ease. Another development was aqueducts. These artificial water passages let the Romans build large cities in areas without nearby water supplies.

Task 1

Sample Response 1

Some students may prefer to take easier classes, but I am convinced that taking challenging classes is better. First of all, students can learn more in challenging classes. The reason is that more difficult classes usually cover more material and have more motivated students. On top of this, taking harder classes makes it easier to get into a good university. Universities are more impressed by students who take harder classes. To me, it is clear that it is better to take harder classes.

Sample Response 2

Many students believe that they should take harder classes. But it is my opinion that taking easier classes is a smart idea. The first reason I feel this way is that challenging classes can be too stressful. Most parents expect their children to get good grades at school. Taking challenging courses makes getting high grades difficult. Then there is the fact that easier classes take up less time. This allows students to do other activities, such as playing sports and practicing music.

Task 2

Listening

03-08

W Student: I'm so pleased that a new dining hall is opening.

M Student: I'm not. Why do we need a three-star restaurant on campus? The prices there will be too expensive for most students.

W: Actually, the prices won't be too high. Students will only have to pay about $10 to eat lunch or dinner there.

M: That's not too bad. But how do you know that?

W: I'm in the Department of Hospitality, so I'm going to be working there.

M: Ah, I see. What are you going to be doing?

W: Some nights, I'll help cook the food. Other nights, I'll help serve it. It's going to be a great way for students in the department to get work experience.

M: That makes sense.

W: Yeah. We can learn about the restaurant business and get paid, too. That will definitely help me get a job after I graduate.

M: Hmm . . . I guess I'll go there sometime. It sounds like a good idea.

Sample Response

The man and the woman are talking about an announcement about a new dining hall. The dining hall will be like a three-star restaurant, and students at the university will work there. The woman is pleased with the announcement. First, she says that it will not be too expensive for students to eat lunch or dinner there. Then, she says that she will work there. She will both cook and serve food. So she will get work experience and be paid. She thinks working there will help her find a job later.

Listening

03-09

Professor: Okay, so you all know what advertisements are. But you might still be wondering how they convince people to buy products . . .

Well, consider a typical example: milk advertisements. Most milk advertisements are directed at women, especially mothers. Advertisers know that mothers want to keep their children happy and healthy. So most milk ads feature images of caring mothers giving milk to their children. The message from this is clear: Good mothers give lots of milk to their children. But that's not all. Milk advertisements also talk about the nutritional benefits of milk. They usually mention something like . . . uh, four out of five doctors recommend drinking a glass of milk each day. By including this information, advertisers can convince mothers to buy lots of milk for their children.

Sample Response

The reading passage gives information on how advertisers create effective advertisements. It states that advertisers research what products customers buy and their reasons for buying them. In her lecture, the speaker talks about milk advertisements. She says that advertisers understand that mothers want their children to be happy and healthy. Therefore, they create milk ads featuring caring mothers giving milk to their children. The ads also mention the health benefits of milk. This convinces mothers to give milk to their children. This example shows how effective advertising meets the expectations of customers.

Listening

03-10

Professor: Animals become used to their environments in a process called adaptation. Some environments require more adaptations than others. So that you can understand this, I want to go over how two animals have adapted to the severe climates of the north.

One animal that is well adapted to extreme cold is the snowy owl. All owls are covered in feathers. But the snowy owl is special. Its coat of feathers is very thick. Not only that, but the feet of snowy owls have also adapted. You see, the snowy owl has heavy feathers on its feet. These adaptations allow the snowy owl to live in areas north of the Arctic Circle.

The arctic wolf also has a couple of interesting adaptations to arctic weather. One such adaptation is its ears. They are smaller and more rounded than those of other wolves. It also has shorter legs and smaller feet. At the same time, it has a bigger body protected by a thick layer of white fur. These adaptations allow the arctic wolf to maintain a higher body temperature. This lets it keep its organs warm even in temperatures as low as forty degrees below zero.

Sample Response

The instructor talks about how animals adapt to extreme climates. He explains this by talking about the snowy owl and the arctic wolf. The snowy owl has a thick coat of feathers as well as feathers on its feet. These adaptations allow the snowy owl to live north of the Arctic Circle. Next, the instructor mentions the arctic wolf. Compared to regular wolves, the arctic wolf has smaller ears and shorter legs. It also has a larger body and thicker fur. As with the snowy owl, these adaptations allow the arctic wolf to survive in extremely cold temperatures.

TOEFL®
MAP
New TOEFL® Edition

Speaking

Basic